SINATRA

HIS LIFE AND TIMES
BY FRED DELLAR

OMNIBUS PRESS
LONDON · NEW YORK · SYDNEY

Copyright © 1995 Omnibus Press
(A Division of Book Sales Limited)

Edited by Chris Charlesworth
Cover & Book designed by Mike Warry, 4i Limited
Picture research by Nicola Russell

ISBN: 0.7119.4978.6
Order No.OP47772

Exclusive Distributors
Book Sales Limited, 8/9 Frith Street,
London W1V 5TZ, UK.

Music Sales Corporation,
257 Park Avenue South,
New York, NY 10010, USA.

Music Sales Pty Limited,
120 Rothschild Avenue, Rosebery,
NSW 2018, Australia.

To the Music Trade only:
Music Sales Limited, 8/9 Frith Street,
London W1V 5TZ, UK.

Photo credits: All pictures supplied by London Features
International except page 56 (left) by Harry Goodwin.
Every effort has been made to trace the copyright holders
of the photographs in this book but one or two were
unreachable. We would be grateful if the photographers
concerned would contact us.

Printed in the United Kingdom by Ebenezer Baylis & Son,
Worcester.

A catalogue record for this book is available from the
British Library.

Author's Note: Few vocalists have altered the course of popular music, changed the way people think, the way they dream. Bing Crosby, Frank Sinatra, Elvis Presley, Bob Dylan certainly. And, if you want, add the names of Louis Armstrong, Billie Holiday, James Brown, Nat Cole and two or three others. But, of these, Sinatra is the only one to have notched chart records in seven decades, from the Thirties right through to the Nineties. Not so prolific in the field of recording these days – hardly unexpected from a man about to extinguish eighty candles on his 1995 birthday pizza – he's nevertheless gigged like crazy in recent times, almost as if Francis Albert feels that, without a microphone in front of him and a crowd outfront to provide added stimulus, he'd end up on the losing end of that big arivederci.

This book is an attempt to log many of Sinatra's achievements. It's not complete, because to notch every live date he ever played would fill a book three times this size. Nevertheless, all the important gigs (and quite a few minor ones) and many TV appearances and radio broadcasts are included, along with a complete run-down of Frank's recording sessions and films, plus a UK discography. Not that such a listing has been achieved without considerable help, this stemming mainly from John Martland, who contributed virtually all the film data, Stan Britt, who was completing his own Sinatra book but still found time to help out on this one, and Ed O'Brien who filled in all remaining gaps. To these friends, along with various members of The Sinatra Music Society, this book is dedicated. **Fred Dellar, April 1995**

All UK chart places are those reported in the NME listing, which was the first of its kind to appear in the UK. American chart placings stem from Billboard.

1915

December 12
Francis Albert Sinatra is born, the son of Natalie Catherine 'Dolly' (Garavante) and Anthony Martin Sinatra of 415 Monroe Street, Hoboken, New Jersey. The baby weighs 13 and a half pounds but during the breech birth the doctor's forceps cause damage to the face and neck, lacerating one ear and puncturing an eardrum. The father, Marty, is a former prizefighter who holds down a job as boilermaker in the local shipyard.

1916

April 2
The four-month baby is christened at St Francis Church.

June
At six months, Frank is placed in the care of his grandmother, Mrs Rosa Garavante, while his mother involves herself in local political activities.

1927

August 1
Marty Sinatra, Frank's father, joins the Hoboken Fire Department.

1930

Summer
The Sinatras go on holiday in the Catskill Mountains.

December 12
Frank receives a ukelele as a 15th birthday present from his uncle Domenico.

1931

January 28
After graduating from David E Rue Junior School, Frank enters Demarest High, and joins the school glee club, becoming the featured singer. But his stay proves problematic for the high school principal and Sinatra lasts just a brief spell at the establishment. Later enrolls at Drake Business School.

December 15
Age 16, he drops out of Drake.

1932

January
The young Sinatra offers to sing with various clubs and bands in the New Jersey area in an effort to further his now chosen career.

March
To supplement his meagre earnings as a singer, Frank takes a menial job with *The Jersey Observer* who pay $11 a week. Not long after, following the death of a colleague, he becomes a sports writer for the paper.

December 31
The Sinatras move into their first home, a four storey, centrally-heated, wooden building at 841 Garden Street, costing a then astronomical $13,400. A local paper reports: "A New Year's party was given in the home of Mrs & Mrs M Sinatra of Upper Garden Street in honour of their son Frank. Vocal selections were given by Miss Marie Roemer and Miss Mary Scott, accompanied by Frank Sinatra."

1934

Summer
While spending a holiday with his aunt, Mrs Josephine Monaco, in Long Branch, New Jersey, Frank meets seventeen year-old Nancy Carol Barbato, a plasterer's daughter. They continue to date and, according to legend, one night hear Bing Crosby at New Jersey's Loew's Journal Square Theater, Bing's performance providing Frank with added incentive to become a singer. He is aided in his ambitions by his mother who buys her son a portable P.A. system, which he loans to bands willing to let him sing with them.

1935

April 26
Frank performs at a ball held by Hoboken's Sicilian Cultural League at the local Union Club, after which he gains brief residency at the Club but quits after falling out with the venue's owner.

September 8
Frank appears on The Major Bowes Amateur Hour as a member of The Hoboken Four, a vocal quartet that has risen out of the ashes of The Three Flashes. The show is broadcast from the stage of New York's Capitol Theater. Proving winners, the Four then move on to play on Bowes' touring show, Frank eventually quitting due to group differences that usually end in fights.

During this period Frank appears in Major Bowes Amateur Theater Of The Air, a filmed short featuring several of Bowes discoveries, Frank appearing with black face in an instrumental group.

1937

May 2
On the *Town Hall Tonight* Show starring Fred Allen, Frank leads The Four Sharps Dixieland jazz outfit through a rendition of 'Exactly Like You'.

August 17
Begins singing with The Harold Arden Band at Englewood, NJ's Rustic Cabin roadhouse. A regular engagement, it initially nets Frank $15 a week, a fee which he still receives eighteen months later.

1938

November 27
Frank is arrested on a morals charge after girlfriend Toni Francke accuses him of making her pregnant. She later withdraws the charge but then accuses him of adultery. Again the charge is dropped. Meanwhile, the job at the Rustic Cabin is providing one distinct advantage in that the owner has a direct line to radio station WNEW and by the end of 1938 Sinatra is performing three to five 15-minute shows each week from WNEW, some in conjunction with an up-and-coming Dinah Shore.

1939

February 3
Frank records a demo titled 'Our Love' with The Frank Manne Orchestra.

February 4
Weds Nancy Barbato at the Catholic Church Of Lady Of Sorrows in Jersey City. Now a considerable attraction at the Rustic Cabin and pulling $25 a week, he rents an apartment at 487 Garfield Avenue, Jersey.

June
Is heard by trumpet-playing big-band leader Harry James while singing on radio station WNEW's *Dance Band Parade* show. James visits the Rustic Cabin and is impressed, eventually signing Sinatra as band vocalist at $75 a week. James suggests that his new vocalist should be billed as Frankie Satin but Sinatra objects to the name change.

June 30
Sinatra joins the current Harry James tour and appears with the band at Baltimore's Hippodrome Theater. He is being paid $75 a week.

July 10
On a James broadcast from Manhattan's Roseland Ballroom, where the band is playing a residency, Frank sings 'If I Didn't Care' and 'The Lamp Is Low'.

July 13
Cuts first record with the James band, the resulting single being 'From The Bottom Of My Heart'/'Melancholy Mood'. The record sells 8,000 copies. Also on this day, the band play an *American Dances* show recorded at New York's Roseland Ballroom by the CBS network for the BBC. Frank sings 'From The Bottom Of My Heart' and 'To You'.

August 10
James broadcasts from New York's Roseland and Frank sings 'My Love For You' and 'This Is No Dream'.

August
George T Simon of *Metronome* magazine hears the James band at Roseland and provides Sinatra's first press notice, praising the band and commenting on "the pleasing vocals of Frank Sinatra, whose easy phrasing is especially commendable."

October
The James band plays Chicago's Hotel Sherman.

December
Major league bandleader Tommy Dorsey hears Sinatra and asks him to sign to his outfit. Though Frank legally still has to complete a two-year contract with Harry James, the trumpet star allows him to go, claiming: "Frank's wife was having a baby and he needed the extra money."

1940

Early January
Frank plays his last date with the James band, in Buffalo, New York. "That night the bus pulled out with all the rest of the boys at about half-past midnight," Sinatra later recalled, "I'd said goodbye to them all and it was snowing. There was nobody around and I stood alone with my suitcase in the snow and watched the tail-lights disappear. Then the tears started and I tried to run after the bus."

January 26
It's Frank's début date with The Tommy Dorsey band – at Rockford, Illinois. He has two solo songs, 'My Prayer' and 'Marie', the latter being a Dorsey hit that had originally featured the voice of Jack Leonard. But the fans yell for more and a version of 'South Of The Border' is pieced together on the spot.

February 1
Chicago. Frank records his first side with Dorsey, 'The Sky Fell Down', singing to an arrangement fashioned by Axel Stordahl. At the same session he also cuts 'Too Romantic'.

February 26
New York. Recording date with Dorsey. The songs 'Shake Down The Stars', 'Moments In The Moonlight', 'I'll Be Seeing You'.

March 2
Dorsey with Sinatra broadcasts from Frank Daly's Meadowbrook, in Cedar Grove, New Jersey.

March 4
New York. Records 'Say It' and 'Polka Dots And Moonbeams'.

March 12
New York. Records 'The Fable Of The Rose' and 'This Is The Beginning Of The End'.

March 13
The Dorsey band begins a four-week engagement at the New York Paramount.

March 25
New York. Records 'Imagination' and 'Yours Is My Heart Alone' but these takes are not released.

March 29
New York. Records 'Hear My Song Violetta', 'Fools Rush In' and 'Devil May Care'.

April 10
New York. Records 'April Played The Fiddle', 'I Haven't Time To Be A Millionaire', 'Imagination' and 'Yours Is My Heart Alone'.

April 23
New York. Records 'You're Lonely And I'm Lonely' , 'Head On My Pillow', 'It's A Lovely Day Tomorrow', and 'East Of The Sun'.

May 23
New York. Records 'All This And Heaven Too', 'Where Do You Keep Your Heart' and 'I'll Never Smile Again'.

June 7
A daughter, Nancy Sandra Sinatra is born to Frank and Nancy at New Jersey's Margaret Hague Hospital.

June 13
New York. Records 'Whispering'.

June 27
New York. Records 'Trade Winds' and 'The One I Love Belongs To Somebody Else'.

July 17
New York. Records 'The Call Of The Canyon', 'Love Lies', 'I Could Make You Care' and 'The World Is In My Arms'.

July 20
Dorsey's recording of 'I'll Never Smile Again', with vocals by an uncredited Sinatra and The Pied Pipers, enters the US charts, reaches No 1 in the US Billboard charts and hangs on for twelve weeks. On the same day 'Imagination' also charts and reaches No 8.

August 29
New York. Records 'Our Love Affair', 'Looking For Yesterday', 'Tell Me At Midnight' and 'We Three'.

September 9
New York. Records 'When You Awake' and 'Anything'.

September 13
'Trade Winds' enters the US charts and reaches No 10.

September 17
New York. Records 'Shadows On The Sand', 'You're Breaking My Heart All Over Again' and 'I'd Know You Anywhere'.

October
The Dorsey band travels to Hollywood to open at the Palladium, a glitzy new dance palace.

October 16
Hollywood. Records 'Do You Know Why ?'

October 17

The Dorsey band's radio show *Fame And Fortune* premières on NBC . It's sponsored by Nature's Remedies laxative tablets. The show features an amateur song-writing contest, all entries being accompanied by an entry form obtainable from any chemist selling Nature's Remedies. But none of the 26 winners will become hits.

October 31

'Our Love Affair' enters the US charts and reaches No 5.

November 11

Hollywood. Records 'Not So Long Ago' and 'Stardust'.

November 22

'We Three' enters the US charts and reaches No 3.

November 24

Frank and The Dorsey Band record 'I'll Never Smile Again' for the soundtrack of *Las Vegas Nights*, a Paramount film starring Constance Moore and Bert Wheeler.

December 27

'Stardust' enters the US charts and reaches No 7.

1941

January 6

New York. Sinatra and The Dorsey Band record 'Oh Look At Me Now' and 'You Might Have Belonged To Another', two of the winning songs in the Nature's Remedies song contest. The resulting Victor single announces "Contest Winner Of Tommy Dorsey's Fame And Fortune Program" on its label.

January 15

New York. Records 'You Lucky People You' and 'It's Always You'.

January 20

New York. Records 'I Tried', 'Dolores', 'Without A Song'.

February 7

New York. Records 'Do I Worry' and 'Everything Happens To Me'.

February 17

New York. Records the two-part 'Let's Get Away From It All'.

March 21

'Oh Look At Me Now' enters the US charts and reaches No 2.

March 28

The film *Las Vegas Nights* is released, featuring Sinatra with The Dorsey Band. Screened at the Paramount, New York, it is supported by a stage show featuring Ian Ray Hutton, The Andrews Sisters and Allan Jones.

April 3

'Do I Worry' enters the US charts and reaches No 4.

April 18

'Dolores' enters the US charts and reaches No 7.

April 25

'Everything Happens To Me' enters the US charts and reaches No 9.

May

A college survey conducted by *Billboard* names Sinatra as the most outstanding Male Band singer in the States. In the *Down Beat* poll he displaces Bing Crosby, winner for the previous four years.

May 2

'Let's Get Away From It All' enters the US charts and reaches No 7.

May 20

The Dorsey Band opens for a summer engagement at the Astor Roof.

May 28

New York. Records 'I Never Let A Day Pass By', 'Love Me As I Am' and 'This Love Of Mine'.

June 27

New York. Records 'I Guess I'll Have To Dream The Rest', 'Free For All', 'You And I' and 'Neiani'.

July 15

New York. Records 'Blue Skies'.

August 19

New York. Records 'Two In Love', 'Violets For Your Furs' and 'Pale Moon'.

August 27

Dorsey begins a three-week run at the New York Paramount.

September

While playing a date in Washington DC Frank tells Tommy Dorsey that he wants to quit the band and go solo. "You've got a contract," he's informed. But Sinatra insists that he will be leaving and gives one year's notice.

September 18

New York. Records 'I Think Of You', 'How Do You Do Without Me?' and 'A Sinner Kissed An Angel'.

September 26

New York. Records another take of 'Violets For Your Furs' and 'The Sunshine Of Your Smile'.

October

The Dorsey Band plays an engagement at the Meadowbrook, New Jersey, then heads back to California for the winter.

October 17

'This Love Of Mine' enters the US charts and reaches No 3.

December 7

Frank and The Dorsey Band are in Hollywood making the film *Ship Ahoy* when the Japanese bomb Pearl Harbour, immersing the USA in World War II.

December 12

'Two In Love' enters the US charts and reaches No 9.

December 22

Hollywood. Records 'How About You'.

1942

January 19

Though still with The Dorsey Band, Frank cuts four solo sides for Bluebird Records, with Axel Stordahl as arranger – 'The Night We Called It A Day', 'The Lamplighter's Serenade', 'The Song Is You' and 'Night And Day'. Stordahl says: "Frank had a room in the Hollywood Plaza on Vine Street. We sat in it all afternoon of a sunny day, playing the sides (on advanced acetate discs) over and over on a portable machine. Frank just couldn't believe his ears. He was so excited."

February 19

Hollywood. The Dorsey recording sessions continue with 'Snootie Little Cutie', 'Poor You', 'I'll Take Tallulah' and 'The Last Call For Love'.

March 9

Hollywood. Records 'Somewhere A Voice Is Calling'.

April 16

New York. Reviewing the film *Ship Ahoy*, featuring The Dorsey Band with Sinatra, one

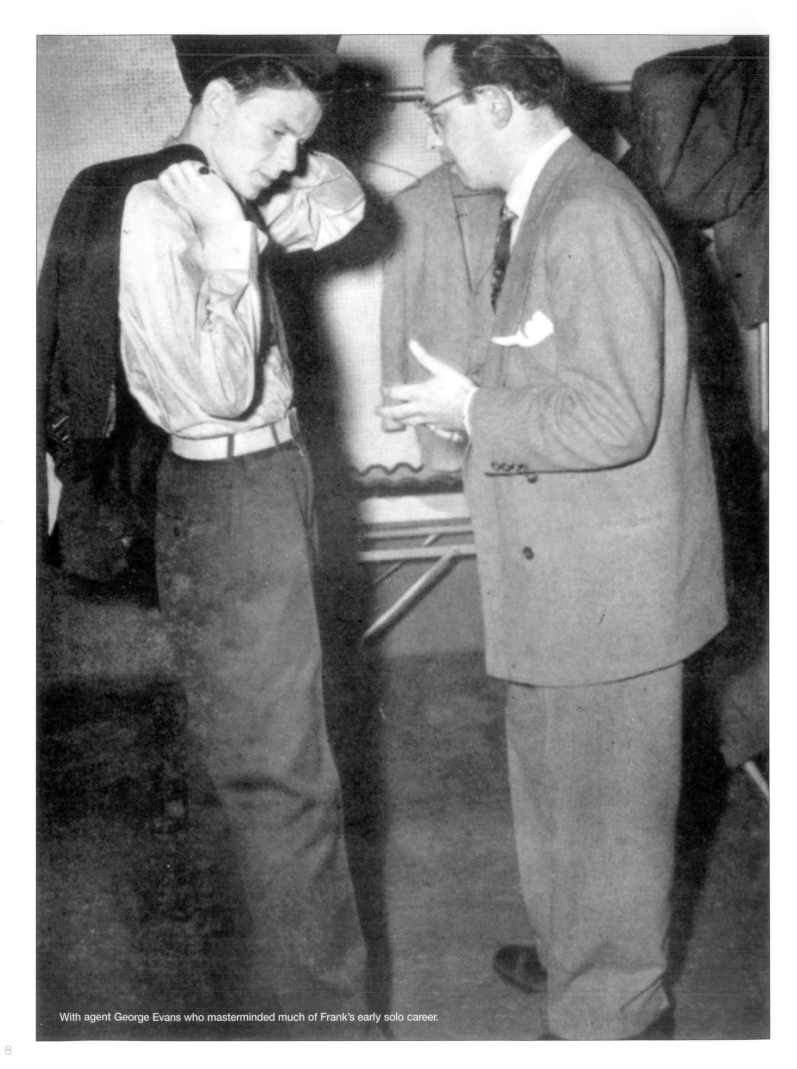

With agent George Evans who masterminded much of Frank's early solo career.

Sinatra (far left) in *Ship Ahoy* with Red Skelton, Eleanor Powell, Tommy Dorsey, Virginia O'Brien and Bert Lahr (centre group)

pundit claims "Dorsey and his Orchestra are around a lot. The music is very good and some of the pieces will be heard in the Hit Parade."

April 18
Dorsey and Sinatra broadcast from Washington's Capitol Theater, sponsored by Raleigh cigarettes.

May 18
New York. Records 'Just As Though You Were Here' and 'Street Of Dreams'.

June 9
New York. Records 'Take Me' and 'Be Careful, It's My Heart'.

June 17
New York. Records 'In The Blue Of Evening', and 'Dig Down Deep' the latter being a plea for citizens to dig deep into their pockets and purchase more War Bonds.

July 1
New York. Records 'There Are Such Things', 'Daybreak' and 'It Started All Over Again'.

July
Frank records 'Light A Candle In The Chapel' with The Dorsey Band. It's his final recording with the band before heading for a solo career.

July 17
'Just As Though You Were Here' enters the US charts and reaches No 3.

August 1
As a protest against the number of jobs being lost to jukeboxes and record-play on radio, American Musicians' Union President James Petrillo orders his members to ban all recording sessions except for those that might help the war effort. No musicians will be allowed to enter a recording studio for many months.

September 18
'Take Me' enters the US charts and reaches No 5.

September 19
Sinatra quits Tommy Dorsey but the break is far from amicable and the singer agrees to provide the bandleader with one third of all his future earnings as a solo act, Dorsey's manager, Leonard Vennerson, claiming another ten percent. It's a high price to pay in order to break his contract. Axel Stordahl also quits Dorsey to become Frank's regular arranger, the singer giving him $650 a week as opposed to Dorsey's $150.

October 29
'Daybreak' enters the US charts and reaches No 10.

November 2
On the *Personal Album* radio show, Frank sings four songs and expounds the value of War Bonds.

November 5
'There Are Such Things' enters the US charts and reaches No 1.

December 30
Benny Goodman begins a four-week stay at the New York Paramount with Peggy Lee, The Radio Rogues and Moke and Poke. Frank is featured as an added attraction, though it's Sinatra, hyped by press agent George Evans, who causes hysteria among the theatre's teen patrons, the press dubbing the phenomena Sinatrauma. Outside the theatre, where the film *Star Spangled Rhythm* is being screened between the onstage show, mobs of girls bring traffic to a standstill. As a result, Frank is held over for another four weeks.

1943

January
Bobbysoxers go wild as Sinatra continues at the Paramount. The singer is becoming the biggest box-office name in America, garnering an incredible amount of newspaper coverage and is dubbed 'The Sultan Of Swoon' and 'Swoonatra' as scores of fans faint after simply hearing his voice.

January 15
Benny Goodman, still smarting from being up-staged by Sinatra at the Paramount, refuses to share the stage with Frank when both entertainers are due to be presented with awards from a fan magazine by actress Madelaine Carroll.

Frank with Ginger Rogers, 1943.

February 4
The film *Reveille With Beverly* is released. Quote: "Fans of jive music will be entertained by Duke Ellington's Orchestra playing 'Take The 'A' Train', Bob Crosby's 'Big Noise From Winnetka' and Freddie Slack's 'Cow Cow Boogie'. In a lighter strain, Frank Sinatra sings 'Night And Day' and The Mills Brothers chip in with two novelty numbers." On the same day 'It Started All Over Again', recorded with Tommy Dorsey, enters the US charts and reaches No 4.

March 17
Manhattan's ritzy Riobamba hosts Sinatra's first night-club appearance. The club is in financial trouble but Frank tells owner Arthur Jarwood "You better start breaking those walls down, Art, I'm going to pack 'em in." The crowds arrive on cue and within five days the club is back in the black.

March 27
Frank replaces Barry Wood as one of the singers on CBS' *Your Hit Parade* series, sponsored by Lucky Strike. The show features America's best selling songs.

May 14
Frank gains his first major starring radio series with *Broadway Bandbox*, a non-sponsored CBS programme in which he and The Raymond Scott Orchestra alternate, Frank providing vocals, Scott the instrumentals. For Sinatra's songs, basically the same band is used but with

added strings and Axel Stordahl conducting. The show will run for six months.

June 7
Now signed to Columbia Records, Frank cuts his first tracks for the label, 'Close To You', 'People Will Say We're In Love' and 'You'll Never Know'. But, due to the musicians' strike, they're *a cappella*, the only accompaniment being provided by The Bobby Tucker Singers.

June 10
Harry James' 'All Or Nothing At All' recorded in 1939 when Sinatra was the band vocalist, enters the US charts and reaches No 2.

June 22
In New York, Frank cuts further sides with The Bobby Tucker Singers – 'Sunday Monday Or Always', 'If You Please' and 'People Will Say We're In Love'. Meanwhile, 'You'll Never Know' enters the US chart and reaches No 2, while the B-side 'Close To You' gets to No 10.

July 1
'In The Blue Of Evening' enters the US charts and reaches No 1. It will be the final Dorsey-Sinatra hit.

July 8
'It's Always You' enters the US chart and reaches No 6.

August 3
Los Angeles police are asked by RKO for 25 police to escort Frank into town later in the month.

August 5
Yet another New York recording session with The Bobby Tucker Singers – another take of

'People Will Say We're In Love' plus 'Oh What A Beautiful Morning', both songs from the Broadway show *Oklahoma*.

August 6
One US national newspaper reports that Frank ranks with Valentino as a 'lady swooner'. He tells gossip columnist Louella Parsons that after finishing the film *Higher And Higher*, George Abbott wants him for the Broadway stage play *The Umpire's Daughter*.

August 12
Frank arrives in California to film *Higher And Higher* and is met at Pasadena station by five thousand teenager screamers.

August 14
Frank plays a concert at the Hollywood Bowl before a crowd of 18,000. Morris Stoloff conducts.

August 30
Jules Stein of MCA buys Frank's contract for $60,000. This means that the singer's ex-boss, Tommy Dorsey, no longer receives a third of Sinatra's earnings. Frank has been paying out a total of 56% of his estimated weekly earnings of $1000 to those who have owned 'a piece of him'.

September 9
'Sunday, Monday Or Always' enters the US charts and reaches No 9, the B-side 'People Will Say We're In Love' settling at No 6.

October 1
Opens for a supper club season in New York's Wedgwood Room at the Waldorf Hotel but only just. For prior to the show, he's so nervy that he slips in his bath, spraining an ankle, nearly forcing him to cancel the show.

October

Frank auctions his old clothes over New York radio station WADC, raising over a thousand dollars in War Bond purchases.

October 17

At the dress rehearsal for the final *Broadway Bandbox* show, Frank records three songs which will appear on V-Discs, a series of records made especially for the Armed Forces. These records are among the first unbreakable vinyl discs to be manufactured, and are shipped to military establishments all over the world.

October 22

Frank is declared fit for military service at a preliminary medical examination.

November 3

The sessions with The Bobby Tucker Singers continue with 'I Couldn't Sleep A Wink Last Night' and 'The Music Stopped'. Both stem from the film *Higher And Higher* in which Frank stars. At a follow-up session on November 10, different takes of the two songs are made.

December 9

Following the discovery that he has a punctured eardrum Sinatra is downgraded to 4F at Newark Induction Center and declared exempt from military service.

November/December

Frank embarks on an East Coast tour with Jan Savitt's Orchestra.

December 27

A newspaper report reveals that girls are going around with bandages on their arms, bearing the legend 'Frankie touched me here'.

1944

January 5

Frank commences a half-hour long nationwide radio series sponsored by Lever Brothers via their Vimms Vitamin division. The Vimms series uses 'This Love Of Mine' as its opening theme. The first show is attended by an invited audience of one – the lucky female being 17-year-old Rita Stearns from Washington D.C. who's won a competition in which she had to describe the singer now known as *The Voice*.

January 10

Frank's son, Franklin Wayne Sinatra, is born at Jersey City's Margaret Hague Maternity Centre.

The 'heart-throb in diapers' weighs 8lb 3 ounces. Frank, who's in Hollywood filming *Step Lively*, hears the news and says he hopes to have six children.

January 12

Frank poses with a portrait of his wife and newly-born son, the picture having been transmitted to the West Coast by Acme Telephoto Service.

January 21

'Music, Fun and Frank Sinatra' run the ads as the film *Higher And Higher* gains a release. The movie hails "The introduction of Frank Sinatra, playing himself with competence and satisfying his most devoted fans. The more discerning among them may notice signs of the young man developing into an engaging light comedian."

February 1

Frank and Bing Crosby appear at Hollywood's Lakeside Golf Club in an exhibition tournament to promote the sale of War Bonds.

February 3

'I Couldn't Sleep A Wink Last Night' enters the US charts and reaches No 5.

February 7

After executives view the first few reels of *Higher And Higher*, Frank signs a seven-year contract with RKO for two films a year. The deal also allows him to make one film a year for another studio.

February 9

"Sinatra Craze Puzzles Britain". Katherine Campbell, head of CBS

in London, says that British fans' response to Frank's recordings is lukewarm and adds that the most popular artists in the UK are Tommy Handley, Beatrice Lillie, Noël Coward and Gracie Fields.

March

Frank returns from Hollywood to spend a few weeks at his Hasbrouck Heights, New Jersey home, but spends some his time persuading Nancy that the family should move to California.

June 7

In honour of daughter Nancy's fourth birthday, Phil Silvers and Jimmy Van Heusen gift her a specially written song, along with all rights. Called 'Nancy (With The Laughing Face)' the song is introduced by Frank on his radio show.

June 13

Sinatra cuts his first vocal tracks for the MGM musical *Anchors Aweigh*.

June 14

The Vimms show reaches its final broadcast.

July 8

Frank sings three Top Ten songs on *Your Hit Parade*, then remains in the studio at KFWB, Los Angeles, to record a special session for V-Discs. He is believed to have recorded eleven songs at the session, seven of which eventually emerge on disc.

July 26

The film *Step Lively* is premièred. "Sinatra plays a small-town Shakespeare, and his singing and Gloria DeHaven's beauty remain the highlights of the show. It proves 'The Voice' is here to stay."

Frank escorts Gloria DeHaven to the premiere of *Step Lively*.

September 28

President Franklin Roosevelt, after whom Frank's son is named, invites the singer to tea at the White House and asks him what is top of the Hit Parade. Sinatra replies 'Amapola'. After seeing a bemused look on the President's face, he later confesses: "I think he thought I was speaking Italian".

October 12

The so-called Columbus Day riot occurs during a return appearance at the Paramount, over 30,000 fans blocking the area around the theatre, requiring a huge number of police to put the area back into working order. "The worst mob scene in New York since nylons went on sale," avers the local police chief. Inside, one Alexander Dorogokupetz scores a hit on Frank with a well-aimed egg and has to be hustled out before fans rip him apart.

October 23

Frank appears on a *For The Record* show, a radio series recorded to provide material for the Armed Forces. One of the songs he performs is 'Dick Todd, Dick Haymes And Como', a re-working of 'Sunday, Monday And Always' dedicated to three of his greatest rivals for the throne occupied by Bing Crosby.

November 10

On the strength of his performance in *Anchors Aweigh*, Frank is signed to a five-year deal by MGM.

November 11

Following a two-year strike, the AFM concludes an agreement with Columbia Records, to whom Sinatra is signed, allowing musicians to return to recording activities once more. For the first time since opting for a solo career, Sinatra will be able to record with an orchestra rather than with just a vocal backing.

November 13/14

With the Musicians Union back at work, Sinatra cuts his initial solo Columbia sides with a real orchestra, led by the ever-present Axel Stordahl. The session produces 'Saturday Night (Is The Loneliest Night Of The Week)', destined to become a worldwide hit, 'There's No You', 'White Christmas' and 'If You Are But A Dream'.

November 25

On the *Transatlantic Spotlight* radio show, with presenters Leslie Mitchell, in London, and Ben Graur, in New York, Frank performs 'Come Out Wherever You Are' and 'These Foolish Things'.

December 1

Frank records 'I Dream Of You', 'I Begged Her', 'What Makes The Sunset' and 'I Fall In Love Too Easily', with Axel Stordahl.

With *It Happened In Brooklyn* co-star Jimmy Durante.

December 3

Another recording session with Stordahl produces 'The Cradle Song', 'Ol' Man River', 'Stormy Weather', 'The Charm Of You' and 'Nancy', the last named being the song co-penned by Phil Silvers and dedicated to Frank's daughter.

December 19

Now in Hollywood, Frank records 'Embraceable You', 'When Your Lover Has Gone', 'Kiss Me Again' and 'She's Funny That Way', with Axel Stordahl.

December 21

'White Christmas' enters the US charts and reaches No 7.

December 30

Frank appears on his last *Your Hit Parade* show, Lawrence Tibbett taking over his spot.

1945

January 18

Frank and Agnes Moorhead appear in *Suspense*, a 25-minute radio drama episode. 'I Dream Of You' enters the US charts and reaches No 7.

January 29

Another Hollywood recording session with Axel Stordahl, this one producing 'My Melancholy Baby', 'Where Or When', 'All The Things You Are' and 'Mighty Lak A Rose'.

February 8

In New Jersey, Frank reports for a further medical to adjudge his eligibility for service in the Armed Forces. "If I get into the army I'd like to be in the Tank Corps," he claims. But after three days on Governor's Island he is rated 2-AF and further disqualified from military service. 'Saturday Night (Is The Loneliest Night Of The Week)' enters the US charts and reaches No 6.

February 15

Frank appears with Bing Crosby, Judy Garland and Bob Hope in *Dick Tracy In B-Flat*, an all-star send-up of strip-cartoon PI Dick Tracy for an Armed Forces Radio Service programme.

February 20

Frank guests on *A Date With Judy*, a CBS radio show in which Judy Garland dreams about Sinatra after watching one of his movies.

March 5

The New Jersey Draft Board claim a mistake has been made and that Frank remains in the 4-F category.

March 6

Hollywood. A recording date, with Stordahl, that creates 'I Should Care', 'Homesick, That's All', 'Dream' and 'A Friend Of Yours'.

May 1

Hollywood and Stordahl once more as Sinatra records 'Over The Rainbow', 'You'll Never Walk Alone', 'If I Loved You' and 'Put Your Dreams Away', a song that Frank uses as a closer on many shows.

May 8

Frank sings two songs on CBS Radio's *VE Day Hollywood Victory Show*, an all-star shindig to celebrate the cessation of hostilities in Europe.

May 16

In Hollywood, Frank records four sides with black gospel group The Charioteers, the session including versions of 'I've Got A Home In That Rock' and 'Jesus Is A Rock (In A Weary Land)', 'Don't Forget Tomorrow Night' and 'Lily Belle'.

May 24

At a New York studio Sinatra cuts two sides ('Stars In My Eyes', 'My Shawl') with Latin-American bandleader Xavier Cugat, who once employed Rita Hayworth in his outfit. 'Dream' enters the US charts and reaches No 7.

Late May

The war in Europe over, Sinatra sets out on a seven-week USO tour to entertain the troops. He is accompanied by comedian Phil Silvers, dancer Betty Yeaton, actress-singer Fay MacKenzie and accompanist Saul Chaplin. In Rome, he is granted an audience with Pope Pius XII who blesses both Frank and some beads for Bing Crosby.

July 10

On *The Chesterfield Supper Club* radio show with Marion Hutton, Frank sings 'How Deep Is The Ocean' and 'There's No You'.

Two scenes from *Anchors Aweigh*.

July 19

Hailed as 'a musical masterpiece' the film *Anchors Aweigh* is released. It stars Sinatra alongside Gene Kelly, as sailors looking for romance while on shore leave, and features a great score. "All the world knows Frank Sinatra can sing. Now it turns out that he can act too!"

July 30

Frank resumes recording with Stordahl in Hollywood, producing 'Someone To Watch Over Me', 'You Go To My Head', 'These Foolish Things' and 'I Don't Know Why'. All of these songs would appear on Frank's first 78 rpm album 'The Voice'.

August 14

Frank is photographed at a radio presentation with a group that includes Orson Welles, Jimmy Durante, Marilyn Maxwell and Janet Blair.

August 22

Hollywood. Frank records 'The House I Live In', 'Day By Day', 'You Are Too Beautiful' and a second version of 'Nancy'.

August 27

The recording session continues with 'America The Beautiful', 'Silent Night', 'The Moon Was Yellow' and 'I Only Have Eyes For You'.

September 9

Frank is reported as saying that he is through with movies, adding "Pictures stink and so do most of the people in them."

September 11

Frank denies the quote and commences a new five-year contract with MGM Pictures.

September 12

A CBS radio series *Songs By Sinatra*, sponsored by Old Gold, gets underway. Axel Stordahl and The Pied Pipers provide back-up.

September 23

On an *Armed Forces Radio Service Command Performance* show, Frank lines up alongside Bing Crosby and Frances Langford.

September 26

A *Songs By Sinatra* show is aired and on it Frank duets with Dinah Shore on 'The Night Is Young And You're So Beautiful' the result gaining a release on V-Disc.

September 30

A Command Performance show with Humphrey Bogart and Lauren Bacall.

November 1

In Gary, Indiana, Sinatra attempts to settle a strike by white students at Froebel High School, who are protesting against the racial integration policies of their new principal. He tells the crowd that he knows all about racial intolerance and was frequently called 'a Mick' when growing up in New Jersey. But local dignitaries are against this attempt at appeasement and though the singer's plea is well-received, the strike continues.

November 9

The House I Live In, a short film advancing the cause of racial harmony, is released. "In story and dialogue, Frank Sinatra makes a simple yet highly effective plea for the advancement of Americanism through the elimination of racial and religious tolerance."

November 10

The *London Evening News* describes Frank as "an undersized man of Italian descent. He has

Bogey with Betty Bacall.

hollow cheeks, sunken eyes, large ears, no chest to speak of; and he has been turned down as unfit for any form of military service."

November 15

New York. Frank records his first session with Mitch Miller, cutting 'Old School Teacher' and 'Just An Old Stone House'.

November 17

Frank receives the American Unity Award mainly for his part in making and appearing in *The House I Live In*.

November 19

Reunited with Stordahl, Sinatra records 'Full Moon And Empty Arms' and 'Oh What It Seemed To Be'.

November 23

Frank guests on the *Bill Stern Radio Show* but doesn't sing.

November 29

'Nancy' enters the US charts and reaches No 10.

November 30

Another Stordahl record date for just one song, 'I Have But One Heart'.

December

MGM release a special, three-minute Christmas trailer in which Frank sings 'Silent Night'.

December 5

Frank conducts an album of melodies composed by Alec Wilder. Tracks 'Air For Oboe', 'Air For Flute' and 'Air For Bassoon'.

Two Franks and a brace of Nancys.

With Gloria Graheme in *It Happened In Brooklyn*.

December 7
Still in New York, Frank records 'A Ghost Of A Chance', 'Why Shouldn't I?', 'Try A Little Tenderness' and 'Paradise'. Stordahl, as usual, is the arranger.

December 10
In New York, Frank completes the Alec Wilder album. Tracks 'Slow Dance', 'Themes And Variations' and 'Air For English Horn'.

December
As the year closes, it's revealed that Frank has made his first million.

1946

January 2
Frank hosts his own *Songs By Sinatra* radio show, sponsored by Old Gold cigarettes. Guest is Peggy Lee. The show's opening theme is 'Night And Day', the closer being 'Put Your Dreams Away'.

January 9
Old Gold Show – guest Lena Romay.

January 16
Old Gold Show – guest Andy Russell.

January 23
Old Gold Show – guest Skitch Henderson.

January 30
Old Gold Show – guest Benny Goodman.

February 3
Hollywood. At a Stordahl date, Sinatra records 'All Through The Day', 'One Love', 'Two Hearts Are Better Than One' and 'How Cute Can You Be?'

February 6
Old Gold Show – guest Bob Hope.

February 13
Old Gold Show – guest Jeannie Carson.

February 14
'Oh What It Seemed To Be' enters the US charts and reaches No 2.

February 24
The recording sessions are continued, Frank waxing 'From This Day Forward', 'Where Is My Bess?', 'Begin The Beguine' and 'Something Old, Something New'.

February 27
Old Gold Show – guest Jimmy Durante.

February 28
'Day By Day' enters the US charts and reaches No 10.

March 6
Old Gold Show – guest Skinnay Ennis.

March 7
Special Oscars are awarded to Sinatra and director Mervyn LeRoy for their part in making *The House I Live In*. During the Awards Ceremony at Grauman's Chinese Theater, Hollywood, Frank sings 'Anywhere', 'I Fall In Love Too Easily' and 'So In Love', all nominated songs. It's the first time that nominated songs are performed on the show.

March 10
Hollywood. More sessions with Stordahl, the

resulting sides being 'They Say It's Wonderful', 'That Old Black Magic', 'The Girl That I Marry', 'I Fall In Love Too Easily', 'How Deep Is The Ocean?' and 'Home On The Range'.

March 13
Old Gold Show – guests The Nat Cole Trio.

March 20
Old Gold Show – guest Van Johnson.

April 7
New York. At a recording session with Axel Stordahl Frank cuts what is intended to be a double-sided 12" single – a version of 'Soliloquy', from the show *Carousel*.

April 10
Old Gold Show – guest Gene Kelly.

April 17
Old Gold Show – guest Shirley Ross.

April 24
Old Gold Show – guests The Slim Gaillard Trio.

May 28
Hollywood. Frank and Axel take a second stab at recording 'Soliloquy' and also record 'Somewhere In The Night', 'Five Minutes More' and 'Could Ja', the last side reuniting Sinatra with The Pied Pipers.

June 19
After an argument with his wife, Frank walks out and heads for New York, two weeks ahead of schedule, to work on the movie *It Happened In Brooklyn*. He attends the Billy Conn-Joe Louis heavyweight fight.

June 20
'They Say It's Wonderful' enters the US charts and reaches No 8.

July 17
Frank arrives in Hollywood from New York for further scenes in *It Happened In Brooklyn* but says he is ill and unable to film.

July 24
Hollywood. More Stordahl arrangements as Sinatra records 'The Things We Did Last Summer', 'You'll Know When It Happens', 'This Is The Night' and 'The Coffee Song'.

July 30
The round of recording continues with 'Among My Souvenirs', 'I Love You', 'September Song', 'Blue Skies' and 'Guess I'll Hang My Tears Out To Dry'. Stordahl arranges.

August 1
'Five Minutes More' enters the US charts and reaches No 1.

August 8
Basically a Christmas recording date as Frank and Axel tackle 'Adeste Fideles', 'Jingle Bells', 'Lost In The Stars' and 'Falling In Love With Love'.

August 22
Hollywood. Another day, another Stordahl recording date, this one producing 'Hush-A-Bye Island', 'So They Tell Me', 'There's No Business Like Show Business' and 'Once Upon A Moonlight Night'.

September 4
Hollywood. Frank, who's filming *It Happened In Brooklyn*, claims he is sick then flies to New York to help out old buddy Phil Silvers, whose long-time stage partner Rags Ragland has died suddenly.

September 5
Sinatra opens at the Copacabana, stooging for Silvers, who feels he cannot play the date without a partner who knows his act. *Variety* calls the event "Inspired".

September 12
Frank attends a publicity photo-shoot for *It Happened In Brooklyn* and also turns up at the soundstage to briefly run through one of the numbers from the film.

October 5
Nancy phones agent George Evans and sobs that Frank has walked out on her.

October 15
Hollywood. A recording date with Stordahl. 'Strange Music', 'Poinciana', 'The Music Stopped', 'Why Shouldn't It Happen To Us?' and 'None But The Lonely Heart' are placed in the can.

October 18
'The Coffee Song' enters the US charts and reaches No 10.

October 23
Frank and Nancy meet at Slapsie Maxie's Hollywood night club and are photographed in seemingly reconciliatory mood. It's Phil Silver's opening night at the venue and Frank appears as a guest artist singing 'Going Home'.

October 24
Hollywood record session. 'Time After Time', 'It's The Same Old Dream', 'I'm Sorry I Made You Cry'. With Stordahl.

October 28
The film musical *Till The Clouds Roll By* is released. An all-star biopic dedicated to the music of Jerome Kern, it features Frank singing 'Ol' Man River'.

October 31
Hollywood recording session. 'None But The Lonely Heart', 'The Brooklyn Bridge', 'I Believe', 'I Got A Gal I Love'. With Stordahl.

November
A three-part profile appears in the *New Yorker*. Penned by E.J. Kahn Jr the series later appears as the first real book on the Sinatra phenomenon.

November 7
Following a morning's work on *It Happened In Brooklyn*, Frank appears on a *Burns and Allen* broadcast. Same day there's another recording session that links Sinatra with Dinah Shore on two songs 'It's All Up To You' and 'My Romance', both Stordahl arrangements. Frank also links with arranger George Siravo for 'All Of Me' and once more gets together with The Pied Pipers for 'The Dum Dot Song', a song about chewing gum that ranks among the worst things he's ever had the misfortune to have thrust in front of him.

December 15
A New York record session with The Page Cavanaugh Trio, considered a white version of the Nat Cole Trio. The songs are 'That's How Much I Love You' and 'You Can Take My Word For It Baby'.

December 17
Frank records 'Sweet Lorraine' with The Metronome All-Stars, a band formed from jazz poll winners. The pianist on the date is Nat Cole. It's the only time that he'll ever appear with Sinatra on an official record date.

December 27
'White Christmas' re-enters the US charts and reaches No 8.

December 29
A Command Performance radio show features Frank plus Jimmy Durante, Carole Landis, Clark Dennis and The Smart Set vocal group.

1947

January 9
Hollywood and another Stordahl recording date. The songs: 'Always', 'I Concentrate On You' and 'My Love For You'.

January 30
Frank requests a permit to buy a gun. He claims he needs it because he frequently carries large amounts of money. As part of his application he is fingerprinted by Sheriff Bob Rogers.

February 11
After flying to Cuba, Frank relaxes at a mansion owned by exiled Mafia boss Lucky Luciano

March 11
Back in Hollywood, Sinatra and Stordahl record 'Ain't Cha Ever Comin' Back' (with The Pied Pipers), 'There But For You Go I', 'Mam'selle' and 'Stella By Starlight'.

March 31
Frank, with Stordahl, records two songs from the show *Brigadoon* – 'There But For You Go I' and 'Almost Like Being In Love'.

April 1
It's announced that Frank will give his salary from his first dramatic role, in *The Miracle Of The Bells*, to sectarian charities.

March 5
The film *It Happened In Brooklyn* is previewed in New York. An inconsequential musical, it stars Sinatra, Kathryn Grayson, Peter Lawford and Jimmy Durante. "Sinatra as a shy Brooklyn boy with a velvet voice, repeats the success of *Anchors Aweigh*. It's heaven for the fans!"

April 9
Sinatra appears in court after columnist Lee Mortimer accuses the singer of striking him at Ciro's, a Hollywood night-club. Sinatra pleads innocent and demands a trial by jury.

April 10
Frank attends a fund raiser for cancer research, held in New York's Times Square.

April 13
Film mogul Jesse L. Lasky decrees that, despite the scuffle with Mortimer, Frank will still play the part of a gentle priest in *The Miracle Of The Bells*.

April 22
Frank announces that he's going into the 'fight racket' and has signed heavyweights Jersey Joe Walcott and Joey Maxim for an outdoor bout in Hollywood.

April 25
Another recording session with Dinah Shore finds the twosome duetting on 'My Romance' and 'Tea For Two'.

May
Frank starts work on *The Kissing Bandit* and gets involved with his all-time most embarrassing film role. But it's goodbye to his involvement on the *Old Gold* Show.

May 9
'Mam'selle' enters the US charts and eventually reaches No 6.

May 10
The single 'Mam'selle' enters the US charts and climbs all the way to No 1.

June
It's a no-no to fight promotion as Frank loses around $50,000 sponsoring the heavyweight tussle between Walcott and Maxim.

June 26 and July 3
Hollywood. Frank records 'Have Yourself A Merry Little Christmas', 'Christmas Dreaming' and 'The Stars Will Remember' with Stordahl.

Frank dons a dog-collar for *The Miracle Of The Bells*.

June 23
Sinatra records 'It All Came True' with Axel Stordahl, a single that will be released only in Britain.

July 27
Frank records 'Embraceable You' for a Lucky Strike promo film.

August
One radio poll adjudges Sinatra as the second most popular person alive. Old adversary Crosby scoops the title, while the Pope runs a poor third.

August 11
Four fine standards are recorded with Stordahl: 'That Old Feeling', 'If I Had You', 'The Nearness Of You' and 'One For My Baby'.

August 17
Hollywood. Stordahl and a recording date that produces 'But Beautiful', 'A Fellow Needs A Girl' and 'So Far'.

Late August
Frank, who earlier engaged portrait artist Bretaine Peters to teach him to paint, donates his first painting, a portrait of a sad clown, for auction in aid of the Jewish Relief Fund. It is purchased by film director Rouben Mamoulian for $750.

September 6
Frank rejoins *Your Hit Parade*. Doris Day is his partner until November 29, after which Beryl Davis becomes the show's other resident singer during Frank's stay with the series.

September 9
Another version of 'It All Came True' is recorded, this time with Alvy West and His Little Band, an outfit that has made a name for itself at New York's Hotel Edison.

October 19
New York. Richard Jones provides the arrangement for 'Can't You Just See Yourself' on a record date that finds Stordahl providing the backing on 'You're My Girl' and George Siravo chipping in a chart for 'All Of Me'.

October 22
New York. A full Stordahl recording date. The songs – 'I'll Make Up For Everything', 'Strange Music', 'Laura' and 'Just For Now'.

October 24
New York. Tony Mottola's trio donates support on a record date that fashions 'My Cousin Louella', 'We Just Couldn't Say Goodbye' and 'S'posin''.

October 26
New York. Sinatra records 'None But The Lonely Heart', 'The Song Is You' and 'Just For Now' with Stordahl.

October 29
New York. A busy recording schedule concludes with cuts of 'Mean To Me', 'Spring Is Here' and 'Fools Rush In'. Stordahl conducts.

October 30
It's declared Sinatra Day in Hoboken, with Sinatra receiving the key to the borough.

November 5 and 9
New York. Recording dates with Axel Stordahl, the songs: 'When You Awake', 'It Never Entered My Mind', 'I'm Glad There Is You', 'Body And Soul' and 'I've Got A Crush On You', the last-named brace of tunes featuring the exquisite trumpet-playing of Bobby Hackett.

November 13
Heading a four week stint at the Capitol Theater, New York, Sinatra befriends supporting artist Sammy Davis Jr.

November 25
New York. Two sides are recorded with Stordahl – 'I Went Down To Virginia' and 'If I Only Had A Match'.

December 4 & 8
Sinatra and Stordahl record 'If I Steal A Kiss', 'Autumn In New York', 'Everybody Loves Somebody', 'Ever Homeward' and the double-sides 'A Little Learnin' Is A Dangerous Thing' on which Frank duets with Pearl Bailey.

December 26, 28 & 30
Back in Hollywood, Sinatra and Stordahl see out the year with sessions that produce: 'But None Like You', 'Catana', 'Why Was I Born?', 'O Little Town Of Bethlehem', 'It Came Upon The Midnight Clear', 'White Christmas', 'For Every Man There's A Woman', 'Help Yourself To My Heart', 'Santa Claus Is Comin' To Town', 'If I Forget You', 'Where Is The One?' and 'When Is Sometime?' The late flurry of recordings is because the American Federation of Musicians is to call a strike and everybody in the industry is stockpiling material in case the dispute proves lengthy.

1948

January 1
As threatened, the AFM goes on strike over contracts with recording companies and Frank's recording activities are, like everybody else's, curtailed. Filmwise, once more emulating Bing Crosby, who won an Oscar playing Father O'Malley in *Going My Way*, Sinatra portrays Catholic priest Father Paul in *Miracle Of The Bells*. But no plaudits are forthcoming.

March 4
The Frank Sinatra Red Cross Radio Show with guest star Beryl Davis.

March 16
Hollywood. With the AFM strike still in force, Frank records 'It Only Happens When I Dance With You' and 'A Fella With An Umbrella', using previously recorded backing tracks.

April 10
Hollywood. The strike-bound Frank is forced to record a cover of Nat Cole's hit 'Nature Boy' in *a cappella* mode with The Jeff Alexander Choir.

May 28
'Nature Boy' enters the US charts and reaches No 18.

June 20
Christina, Frank and Nancy's third child, is born at the Cedars Of Lebanon Hospital, in Hollywood. Frank drives his wife to the hospital at two in the morning, heading through any en route red lights.

August
Work begins on the movie *Take Me Out To The Ball Game*.

November 17
The film *The Kissing Bandit*, a romantic comedy starring Frank and Kathryn Grayson is previewed by *Variety* in Hollywood... "Intended as a cross between satire and whimsy, somehow the ingredients have failed to jell into solid entertainment." Which is putting things kindly.

December 6
With the musicians' recording ban over, Frank and Axel Stordahl resume business cutting the corny 'Sunflower', a hayseed hoedown that sounds like a ringer for the later 'Hello, Dolly!'

December 14
In New York, Frank records 'Once In Love With

Amy' with piano accompaniment, then heads for the West Coast.

December 15
Mitchell Ayers overdubs an orchestral track onto 'Once In Love With Amy'. That same day, in Hollywood, Frank cuts 'Why Can't You Behave?' and 'Bop Goes My Heart' with The Phil Moore Four.

December 19
Hollywood. More Stordahl sessions that result in such tracks as 'Comme Ci Comme Ca', 'No Orchids For My Lady' and 'While The Angelus Was Ringing'.

1949

January 4
Hollywood. The songs 'If You Stub Your Toe On The Moon' and 'Kisses And Tears' are recorded with The Phil Moore Four.

February 28
Hollywood. At a Stordahl session Frank records 'Some Enchanted Evening' and 'Bali Hai' both from the musical *South Pacific*.

March 3
Hollywood. A recording session with Stordahl, the songs – 'Night After Night' and 'The Right Girl For Me', the latter being the only decent song stemming from *Take Me Out To The Ball Game*.

March 9
The movie *Take Me Out To The Ball Game*, starring Frank and Gene Kelly, gains a New York preview. In Britain it later appears as *Everybody's Cheering*. Meanwhile, Frank begins work on a new film, *On The Town*.

April 10
Frank goes R&B and cuts 'The Hucklebuck' with George Siravo. The tune originally mutated from Charlie Parker's bop anthem 'Now's The Time' but became an R&B hit in the hands of Paul Williams. Herbie Haymer contributes the booting sax on the Sinatra version. Also on the same date Frank records the more sedate 'It Happens Every Spring'.

May
Frank and the *Your Hit Parade* show part company, he claims it's due to the paucity of the material he's forced to sing on the programme.

May 6
Frank records a duet with Doris Day 'Let's Take An Old Fashioned Walk' and adds a solo track 'Just One Way To Say I Love You', Axel Stordahl is the arranger.

May 29
After being fired from the film *Annie Get Your Gun* due to drink and drug taking, Judy Garland is hospitalised. Frank telephones her daily.

June 10
'The Hucklebuck' enters the US charts and reaches No 10.

July 10
New York. Using arrangements by George Siravo and Sy Oliver (the latter like Sinatra an ex-Dorsey-ite), Frank records 'It All Depends On You', 'Bye Bye Baby' and 'Don't Cry Joe'.

July 14
New York. Hugo Winterhalter conducts as Frank records 'Every Man Should Marry', 'Just A Kiss Apart' and 'If I Ever Love Again'.

July 21
Hollywood. At this recording session, the arrangements come courtesy of Morris Stoloff, once musical mogul at Columbia Pictures. Apart from a second stab at 'Every Man Should Marry', Sinatra also records the truly dreadful 'The Wedding Of Lili Marlene'.

August
An album, 'Frankly Sentimental' is released but doesn't sell spectacularly well.

September 5
Frank heads a new prime time, 15-minute radio show *Light Up Time*, The sponsor is Lucky Strike cigarettes. However, Axel Stordahl doesn't conduct on the new series, *Down Beat* reporting that the sponsors didn't want to pay his fee.

September 15
At a Hollywood session, Frank records 'That Lucky Old Sun', 'Mad About You' and 'Stromboli' with the Jeff Alexander Orchestra.

October 30
Hollywood. With Axel Stordahl and The Modernaires vocal group, Frank records 'That Old Master Painter' and 'Why Remind Me?'.

November 8
Hollywood. The Stordahl-Modernaires sessions continue with 'Sorry', 'Sunshine Cake' and 'Sure Thing'.

December 8
Frank attends the New York opening of *Gentlemen Prefer Blondes*, a Broadway musical based on Anita Loos' book, in the company of vivacious movie queen Ava Gardner. As a girl, in Newport News, Virginia, Ava had seen him play a date with Tommy Dorsey. "He was my dream idol before we had our first date," she later claimed.

December 9
On The Town, starring Sinatra, Gene Kelly and Jules Munshin attracts rave reviews. A movie musical about three sailors on 24-hour leave in New York, it's nigh faultless, with great songs and outstanding dance routines. But MGM, unhappy with Sinatra, have demoted his name to second billing.

1950

January
Frank and Ava Gardner become an increasingly newsworthy item when they attend a Palm Springs party together.

January 12
Hollywood. Frank and Axel Stordahl record 'God's Country' (featuring a trumpet solo by Ziggy Elman), 'Chattanooga Shoe Shine Boy' and 'Sheila', the last named being banned in Australia where the term 'Sheila' wasn't deemed complimentary.

January 27
Frank begins a two-week residency at The Shamrock Hotel, Houston, Texas.

January 28
George Evans, Frank's long-time press agent, dies from a heart attack, age 48.

February 14
It may be St. Valentine's Day but love is not in the air as Nancy announces that she and Frank have separated.

February 23
Frank cuts 'Kisses And Tears' as a duet with Jane Russell, bosomy star of *The Outlaw* and one-time band singer with Kay Kyser. Also recorded on the date is the solo 'When The Sun Goes Down'.

March 10
New York. A recording date with Mitch Miller that produces' American Beauty Rose', one of

Ava the goddess.

gains a five-year contract with CBS worth a quarter of a million dollars a year.

June 28
A record session in New York finds Frank covering 'Goodnight Irene', a Leadbelly song that's been a hit for The Weavers, along with 'Dear Little Boy Of Mine'. The accompaniment is by Mitch Miller, his Orchestra and Singers.

July 2
Ava joins Frank at his Berkeley Square bachelor flat in London where he is booked to perform his first-ever UK dates.

July 10
Sinatra opens at the London Palladium for a two-week stint, playing two performances each night (6.15 and 8.45 pm) along with matinée dates (2.40 pm) on Wednesdays and Thursdays. Also on the bill are The Skyrockets Orchestra, sand-dancers Wilson, Keppel and Betty,

the few gigs on which Sinatra received a Dixieland jazz backing.

March 28
Frank opens at the Copacabana, New York, for a three-week stint, his first club date in five years. Ava Gardner attends and recalls: "Frank was nervous before he went on, which was unlike him, but he sang like an angel."

April 8
New York. An arrangement by George Siravo and a duet with Rosemary Clooney on 'Peachtree Street'. At the same recording date, Frank also cuts a version of 'There's Something Missing' which is not released.

April
George Siravo provides the arrangements on a series of recording dates that will result in Frank's first long-playing album. Titled 'Sing And Dance With Frank Sinatra', it's also the first of his 'swinging' sessions. Though Sinatra was in the studio for these dates, Mitch Miller claims that Frank's voice was often in such bad shape that he'd cut off the mike and merely record the backing tracks. Later he instructs Sinatra to return to the studio at midnight and other times

when MU representatives are not around, adding vocals by means of overdubs. The dates are allegedly kept secret because tracking is frowned upon by the Union.

April 26
During a show at the Copacabana, Frank opens his mouth to sing and nothing happens. Suffering from an affliction that strangles the vocal chords, he's ordered by his doctor to stop singing for forty days.

April 27
More problems as MGM and Frank call it a day, a somewhat deceptive joint statement from the film company and MCA, Sinatra's agency, announcing: "As a freelance artist, he is now free to accept unlimited, important personal appearance, radio and television offers that have been made to him."

May 11
Frank joins Ava Gardner in Spain where she is filming *Pandora And The Flying Dutchman*.

May 27
Frank makes his television début on Bob Hope's NBC *Star Spangled Revue* and, as a result,

Maudie Edwards, Virginia Lee and comedian Max Wall. Two tall redheads anger Frank by tearing off his bow-tie as he arrives at the theatre, which is thronged by 800 teenagers held at bay by 16 policemen. Inside, Sinatra croons 15 songs to an appreciative audience.

July 22
Frank's last night at the Palladium, where he will be followed by Donald Peers.

July 28
'Goodnight Irene' enters the US charts and reaches No 12.

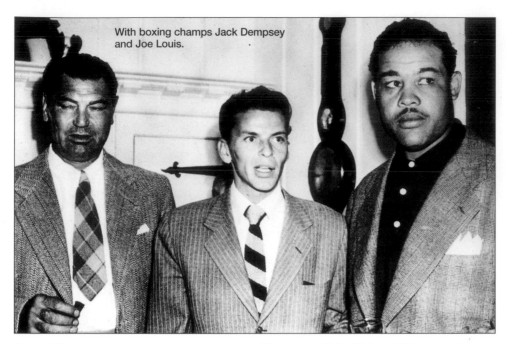

With boxing champs Jack Dempsey and Joe Louis.

August 2
New York. A one-song record session with Percy Faith results in 'Life Is So Peculiar'.

September 18/21
New York. A brace of Stordahl record dates provides 'Accidents Will Happen', 'One Finger Melody', 'Remember Me In Your Dreams', 'If Only She'd Look My Way', 'Meet Me At The Copa' and 'London By Night'.

September 27
Frank and Ava attend the Joe Louis-Ezzard Charles heavyweight fight at New York's Yankee Stadium.

October 7
Frank's CBS TV series kicks-off with a live show that's sponsored by Bulova Watches. But it proves a flop.

October 9
New York. A recording session with Axel Stordahl results in a gorgeous version of 'Nevertheless', with Billy Butterfield on trumpet, plus 'Come Back To Sorrento', 'I Guess I'll Have To Dream The Rest' and 'April In Paris'.

November 5
New York. George Siravo provides the chart on a recording date that produces 'Let It Snow, Let It Snow, Let It Snow'.

November 7
The movie *Double Dynamite*, a comedy in which Frank plays a bank clerk accused of theft, is previewed. "The trio of Frank Sinatra, Jane Russell and Groucho Marx is hard to beat."

November 16
New York. A record session with Stordahl.

The songs – 'Take My Love', 'I Am Loved', 'You Don't Remind Me' and 'You're The One'.

December 11
A second record date with Rosemary Clooney, the twosome waxing 'Love Means Love' and 'Cherry Pies Ought To Be You' but ditching some of Cole Porter's more risqué lines on the latter.

1951

January 16
Two Axel Stordahl arrangements – 'Faithful' and 'You're The One', plus one by George Siravo, 'There's Something Missing', figure on a New York recording session.

January 20
Frank's single 'If Only She'd Look My Way' and 'London By Night' gains a UK release. A charity affair in aid of the British Playing Fields' Association, it contains a short introduction by the Association's president, The Duke of Edinburgh.

February 2
New York. With Axel Stordahl, Frank records two songs from *The King And I*, 'Hello Young Lovers' and 'We Kiss In A Shadow'.

March 27
Frank records 'I'm A Fool To Want You', a song that he co-wrote. It is dedicated to Ava Gardner. On the same Stordahl session, he cuts 'I Whistle A Happy Tune' and 'Love Me'.

May
In a month designated 'Frank Sinatra Record Month', American DJ's invite their listeners to vote for their favourite Sinatra songs, some of which will be used in the upcoming movie *Meet Danny Wilson*.

May 10
This is it, the legendary session that would lead to Sinatra and Columbia parting company. Mitch Miller asks Sinatra to record a song called 'Mama Will Bark' with Dagmar a comedienne (i.e. she caused laughs) of Amazonian proportions. A novelty to end all novelties, 'Mama Will Bark' included dog impressions and Sinatra making noises like Jimmy Durante. "The only ones who bought were dogs," Sinatra later complained. At the same session he also records 'It's A Long Way From Your House To My House'. But not a lot of people remember that.

May 29
Nancy announces that she and Frank are splitting up: "I am now convinced that divorce is the only way for my happiness as well as Frank's. It is better for the children too."

June 9
CBS-TV air the last show in Frank's first TV series.

June 21
A recording session with Shelley Winters finds the duo working their way through 'A Good Man Is Hard To Find', once recorded by Bessie Smith.

July 19
There's a studio reunion with old boss Harry James to record three songs: 'Farewell, Farewell To Love', 'Deep Night' and 'Castle Rock', the last named proving, lyrically, a swing-era forerunner of 'Rock Around The Clock'.

August 19
A mustachioed Frank is photographed alongside Ava at Reno's Riverside Hotel. He is playing a singing engagement at the venue as well as fulfilling a six months' residency requirement for a Nevada divorce.

August 31
Lake Tahoe. It's reported that Frank has taken an overdose of sleeping pills following a tiff with Ava Gardner, but he denies any attempt at suicide.

September 28
In California, Nancy Sinatra takes the witness stand as she applies for a degree of separate maintenance which will entitle her to around a third of Frank's earnings. The action is uncontested.

October 9

Frank's second season on CBS-TV gets underway.

October 30

Nancy is granted a divorce and wins a third of her ex-husband's annual income plus ownership of the Holmby Hills house, along with custody of the children. Meanwhile, Frank and Ava immediately apply for a marriage licence in Philadelphia.

November 2

Frank and Ava arrive back in New York and are snapped by photographers at Pennsylvania Station.

November 7

Sinatra and Ava Gardner wed at the Philadelphia home of old friend Manie Sacks, the man who had originally recommended Frank to Harry James. Axel Stordahl is best man, and singer June Hutton, Axel's wife, is maid of honour. Approximately sixty guests are present, not counting the body of reporters and photographers who cluster outside the house, receiving little but abuse. Inside, Mendelssohn's wedding march sounds a little strange due to an untuned piano. After the ceremony, the couple are driven to the airport in a limo, eventually taking a plane to Miami, before moving on to Havana, Cuba.

November 14

Frank and Ava attend a film preview and are photographed in the company of Dolly and Marty Sinatra.

December 9

Ava joins Frank onstage at the London Coliseum during a midnight charity performance in aid of the Playing Fields' Association.

December 18

The semi-autobiographical movie *Meet Danny Wilson* is previewed in Hollywood. "The resemblance to Sinatra's own career is more than passably noticeable. But the singer's TV activities may be cutting into his box office value."

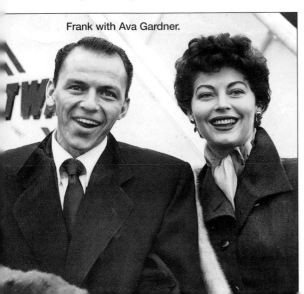

Frank with Ava Gardner.

1952

January 1

CBS-TV and Echo present *The Frank Sinatra Show* with Louis Armstrong, The Three Stooges and Yvonne DeCarlo,

January 7

With relations between Frank and Columbia A&R man Mitch Miller at an all-time low, Sinatra begins his last year with Columbia Records, cutting such sides as 'I Could Write A Book', 'I Hear A Rhapsody' and 'Walkin' In The Sunshine' at a Hollywood studio.

February 6

Hollywood. Frank records 'My Girl', 'Feet Of Clay' and 'Don't Ever Be Afraid To Go Home' with Axel Stordahl.

Jerry Lewis.

March 15

Dean Martin and Jerry Lewis host a telethon on behalf of the Muscular Dystrophy Association and other causes. Among the host of stars on the show is Frank Sinatra. It's the first time he's ever worked with Dean Martin.

March 26

Frank makes an emotional return to the New York Paramount for a series of shows. The theatre is screening *Meet Danny Wilson*. But the New York World Telegram reports that the second balcony, which seats 750, is empty and that the term 'Frankie', to the girls at the stage door, meant Frankie Laine.

April 1

CBS screen the final show in Frank's second TV series.

June 3

A diverse recording session in Hollywood, conducted by Stordahl, finds Frank delivering a killer 'Birth Of The Blues' and an equally bluesy 'Azure Te', along with a brash R&B influenced 'Bim Bam Baby', 'Tennessee Newsboy', a country music shuffle, and a perfunctory Italian ballad 'Luna Rossa'.

June 29

Judy Garland is 'roasted' by the Friar's Club at L.A.'s Biltmore Bowl, where Frank sings 'Dear Miss Garland, You Made Us Love You'.

September 17

Frank's parting shot. His last recording date for Columbia is 'Why Try To Change Me Now?' with Percy Faith conducting.

September

The singer plays a hometown Fireman's Ball gig at the Hoboken Union Club but has a bad night.

October 18

Depressed, Frank fights with Ava and argues with Lana Turner.

October 27

At the Hollywood Palladium Frank and Ava Gardner appear at a film stars' rally in support of Adlai Stevenson's presidential candidacy. Frank sings 'The House I Live In' and 'The Birth Of The Blues'.

November 7

The Sinatras fly to Nairobi, where Ava is to film *Mogambo*, the duo celebrating their wedding anniversary aboard a plane.

November 14

Hollywood. Sinatra screen-tests for the part of Angelo Maggio in the projected movie *From Here To Eternity*, based on the Pearl Harbour-era novel by James Jones. Eli Wallach, who already tests for the part, seems a shoo-in but has to duck out due to other commitments.

Late November

Ava visits a London clinic and is told that she is pregnant. She opts for an abortion.

Clark Gable and Grace Kelly.

December 13

Frank returns to Africa to spend Christmas with Ava who is filming *Mogambo* with Clark Gable and Grace Kelly. During this period, Ava becomes pregnant yet again. Later she confesses: "I reached the same decision about my second pregnancy as I had about my first."

December 31

The contract with Columbia Records reaches termination point.

1953

March 2

Shooting begins in Hollywood for *From Here To Eternity*.

April 2

Frank records his first-ever session for Capitol Records. Voyle Gilmore produces, Axel Stordahl provides the arrangements and four songs are cut: 'I'm Walking Behind You', 'Don't Make A Beggar Out Of Me', 'Day In, Day Out' and 'Lean Baby', the last-named being a vocal cover of a Billy May hit.

April 30

With Axel Stordahl heading out to become MD on Eddie Fisher's *Coke Time* TV series, Sinatra is linked with arranger Nelson Riddle for a session that produces 'I've Got The World On A String', 'Don't Worry About Me', 'I Love You' and 'South Of The Border'. The last two songs are arranged in a style resembling that of Billy May and actually receive a label credit as being by 'Billy May and his Orchestra'.

May 2

Los Angeles. A recording session with Nelson Riddle. The songs – 'Anytime, Anywhere', 'My One And Only Love', 'From Here To Eternity' and 'I Can Read Between The Lines'.

May

Sinatra mounts a month-long tour of Europe and newspaper reports suggest that some of his concerts are badly attended. Later the singer claims: "The report of the concert in Helsinborg was inaccurate. The attendance was not 4,000 but 15,000 and I sang not for 32 minutes but for 80 minutes." Criticised for drinking tea onstage during a concert at Malmo ("Crosby must have made this tea") Frank claims that he didn't know it was to be an open-air gig and that he was cold. "I drank the tea after singing 'Ol' Man River', it's a song that takes a lot of singing. I'm sorry if some of the audience felt insulted." He also adds that, "While we were going into one hotel in Sweden, the hotel manager saw my accompanist Bill Miller and British conductor Harold Collins about to register and stopped them, saying: 'We don't want any gangsters here'."

June 14

Frank's UK tour opens with two concerts at the Granada, Tooting. The *NME* reports "Sinatra has changed a lot from the shy guy whom America knew in the mid-'40s. Soberly attired in a dark lounge suit and minus the famous bow tie, he is now sophistication personified and blessed with a dry ad lib wit." His programme includes 'September Song'. 'Don't Worry About Me', 'You Go To My Head', 'Tenderly', 'Ol' Man River', 'That Old Black Magic ("I think that would make a great song for Billy Daniels"), 'Sweet Lorraine', 'One For My Baby', 'I'll Never Smile Again' and 'Birth Of The Blues'. Billy Ternent's Orchestra supplies back-up on the whole tour.

June 15

Commences a week in variety at Bristol Hippodrome.

June 18

Frank sings to the patients at Bristol Women's Hospital.

June 21

Concert: Kilburn State cinema.

June 25

Interviewed on BBC radio by Joan Gilbert.

June 28

Concert: Edmonton Regal.

June 29:

Commences a week in variety at Birmingham Hippodrome.

July 5

Concert: Elephant and Castle Trocadero.

July 6

Commences a week in variety at Glasgow Empire.

July 11

BBC radio *Show Band Show* with compère Rikki Fulton and The Stargazers vocal group. Frank's fee for the show is donated to the Variety Club Of Great Britain's Heart Fund.

July 12

Concert: Caird Hall, Dundee.

July 13

Concert: Edinburgh.

July 16

A second appearance on the BBC Show *Band Show*.

July 20

Commences a week in variety at The Palace, Manchester.

July 23

The film *From Here To Eternity* is previewed. "With the release of this film, a personality is re-born. It's a smash screen adaptation of the James Jones best-seller and Sinatra scores a decided hit as Angelo Maggio, a violent, likeable, Italo-American GI."

July 26

A concert at the Blackpool Opera House provides a widely available bootleg.

July 30

Commences a week in variety at the Liverpool Empire.

August 9

Frank's last concert of his British tour – at

Ernest Borgnine and Burt Lancaster square-up in *From Here To Eternity*.

London's Hammersmith Commodore. Prices 4/6 to 10/6.

August 11

Sinatra flies out after penning a note (published in *NME*) that reads: "Farewells are never pleasant and with my flight tonight to America, I feel "the sweet sorrow" of parting. I have been accorded a wonderful welcome during my tour of these beautiful Isles and will carry home a legion of memories."

October

Frank plays a season at the Sands Hotel, Las Vegas. NBC begins broadcasting *Rocky Fortune*, a 25-minute, weekly drama series starring Sinatra in the title role.

October 27

MGM announce that Sinatra and Ava Gardner have separated and that she will be seeking a divorce.

November 5/6

In LA Frank records tracks for the 'Songs For Young Lovers' LP with Nelson Riddle, 'A Foggy Day', 'My Funny Valentine', 'They Can't Take That Away From Me', 'Violets For Your Furs', 'Like Someone In Love', 'I Get A Kick Out Of You', 'Little Girl Blue' and 'The Girl Next Door'.

November 18

It's reported that Frank has cut his wrists and been taken to Mt Sinai Hospital.

Late November

The *To Be Perfectly Frank* radio shows begin on NBC. These 15-minute spots, with a small group or with pianist Bill Miller, will be broadcast twice a week through to Spring 1955.

December 8/9

Two Los Angeles recording sessions with Riddle produce 'Take A Chance', 'Ya Better Stop', 'Why Should I Cry Over You?', 'Rain (Falling

From The Skies)', 'I Could Have Told You' and 'Young At Heart'.

December 23

Frank joins Ava in Madrid for Christmas.

1954

January 12

It's announced that Frank will be heard but not seen in the 20th Century Fox picture *We Believe In Love*, in which he'll sing 'Three Coins In The Fountain' receiving $10,000 (roughly £3,500) for this brief performance. The film will later be renamed *Three Coins In The Fountain*.

Frank teams with Doris Day for *Young At Heart.*

February 13
The single 'Young At Heart' enters the US charts and remains there for 22 weeks, peaking at No 2.

March 1
Los Angeles. A recording session with Nelson Riddle produces three songs -'Day In Day Out', 'Last Night When We Were Young' and 'Three Coins In The Fountain'.

March 16
The final episode in the *Rocky Fortune* radio series is broadcast by NBC.

March 25
Frank receives an Oscar from Mercedes McCambridge as Best Supporting Actor for portraying Maggio in *From Here To Eternity*. The winner claims: "If I start thanking everybody, I'll do a one-reeler... they're doing a lot of songs up here but nobody asked me. I love you though." Both Nancy Jr and Frank Jr turn up but Ava fails to show.

April 2
In Los Angeles Frank records 'The Sea Song' with Nelson Riddle. The record is not released.

April 7 & 19
The 'Song For Young Lovers' album is pieced together, Frank and Nelson Riddle recording 'Sunday', 'Just One Of Those Things', 'I'm Gonna Sit Right Down And Write Myself A Letter', 'Wrap Your Troubles In Dreams', 'All Of Me', 'Jeepers Creepers', 'Get Happy' and 'Taking A Chance On Love'.

May 11
L.A. With Nelson Riddle, Frank records 'The Gal That Got Away','Half As Lovely (Twice As True)' and 'It Worries Me'.

May 26
Frank has his second big single of the year as 'Three Coins In The Fountain' enters the US charts and reaches No 7.

July 10
The single 'Young At Heart' reaches No 12 in the UK chart.

August 23
L.A. Another session with Riddle produces 'When I Stop Loving You', 'White Christmas' and 'The Christmas Waltz'.

August 30
The movie *Suddenly*, in which Frank teams with Sterling P. Hayden, James Gleason and Nancy Gates, is previewed. "It's an unusual exploitation yarn in which Sinatra does a wonderful job as a professional gunman hired to kill the President as he debarks from his special train."

September 18
'Three Coins In The Fountain' reaches No 2 in the UK singles chart.

September 23
L.A. With Nelson Riddle, Frank records 'Don't Change Your Mind About Me', 'Someone To Watch Over Me' and 'You My Love'.

November 5
Frank drives Joe DiMaggio to an apartment where, with other friends and two private detectives, DiMaggio, seeking evidence to use in a divorce case, breaks in, hoping that he will find evidence of a suspected lesbian relationship. But the raid goes awry and the wrong apartment is entered. Frank later admits that he drove DeMaggio to the scene of the raid but claims he took no further part in the escapade.

November 20
Frank begins recording the soundtrack to *Finian's Rainbow*, an animated cartoon version of the Lane-Harburg show, cutting an ad-lib blues with Louis Armstrong, along with a version of 'Necessity' with Ella Fitzgerald.

December 2
A further *Finian's Rainbow* session produces a version of 'Old Devil Moon', with Ella Logan.

December 7
The film *Young At Heart* is previewed in Hollywood. "The teaming of Frank Sinatra and Doris Day would seem like box-office gold in this smoothly fashioned production which is based on the 1938 Claude Rains/John Garfield movie *Four Daughters*."

December 9
Frank records 'If This Isn't Love' for *Finian's Rainbow*. Later, another punch-up is reported as Frank and friends leave the Crescendo, Hollywood, after seeing Mel Torme onstage. This time, Torme's publicist Jim Byron claims to be on the receiving end.

December 10-11
Another *Finian's Rainbow* session produces 'Necessity' and 'Great Come And Get It Day'. But though Frank (cast as Woody) records the narration for the film, the project is later shelved.

December 13
L.A. Sinatra records with the Ray Anthony Orchestra, cutting 'Melody Of Love' and 'I'm Gonna Live Till I Die'.

December
Frank accompanies heiress Gloria Vanderbilt to a Broadway opening, sparking rumours of a romance.

As Maggio in *From Here To Eternity*.

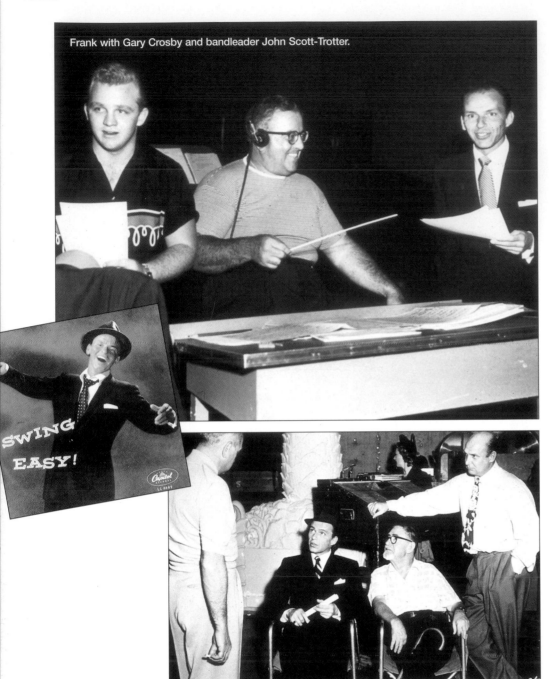

Frank with Gary Crosby and bandleader John Scott-Trotter.

On the *Joker's Wild* set.

1955

February 8, 16 & 17
L.A. Frank and Nelson Riddle record tracks for the 'In The Wee Small Hours' album. Songs: 'Dancing On The Ceiling', 'Can't We Be Friends', 'Glad To Be Unhappy', 'I'll Be Around', 'What Is This Thing Called Love?', 'Ill Wind', 'I See Your Face Before Me', 'Mood Indigo', 'I Get Along Without You Very Well', 'In The Wee Small Hours Of The Morning', 'When Your Lover Has Gone', 'This Love Of Mine'.

February 21
Los Angeles. A recording of 'Soliloquy' is attempted but not completed.

March 4
At a further 'Wee Small Hours' session, 'It Never Entered My Mind', 'Deep In A Dream' and 'I'll Never Be The Same' are completed, along with the single 'Not As A Stranger'.

March 7
L.A. With Nelson Riddle Frank records 'If I Had Three Wishes' and 'How Could You Do A Thing Like That To Me?' then cuts two rock sides with Dave Cavanaugh and The Nuggets, 'From The Bottom To The Top' and 'Two Hearts, Two Kisses', the latter being a cover of an R&B hit.

March 23
L.A. Frank and Riddle record 'Learnin' The Blues'.

March 28
Together, Lauren Bacall and Sinatra visit Judy Garland at the Cedars Of Lebanon Hospital, where Judy is to give birth to a son, Joey Luft.

March 30
At RKO Pantages Theater, Hollywood, Frank makes the award of Best Supporting Actress to Eva Marie Saint (*On The Waterfront*) during the annual Oscar event. 'Three Coins In The Fountain' takes the Best Song plaudit.

April 4
'Learnin' The Blues' enters the US charts and reaches No 2.

April 25
LP 'In The Wee Small Hours' released. It's his first 12" album (not in Britain where it later arrives as two 10" releases) and contains a series of immaculately performed and arranged love songs.

May 30
Frank captures a suspected burglar at his home in Palm Springs with a flying tackle and detains the man until the police arrive.

June
Frank learns that actor Lee J Cobb has suffered a heart attack and rushes to his bedside. Cobb, a victim of black-listing by the Un-American Activities lobby, is broke. But Frank pays all his hospital bills and helps support Cobb's two children.

Robert Mitchum.

June 10
Not As A Stranger, in which Sinatra portrays a struggling medical student, gets a New York preview... "Frank Sinatra is particularly splendid in this operating room drama, which also co-stars Robert Mitchum, Olivia de Havilland, Broderick Crawford and Gloria Grahame."

June 11
'You My Love' reaches No 13 in the UK singles chart.

The guys in *Guys and Dolls*.

Brando as Sky Masterson and Frank as Nathan Detroit in *Guys and Dolls*.

July 29

L.A. With Nelson Riddle, Frank records 'Look To Your Heart', 'Love And Marriage', 'The Impatient Years' and 'Our Town', the four songs stemming from the forthcoming NBC-TV musical version of Thornton Wilder's play *Our Town*, featuring Sinatra as narrator.

August

Frank and Nancy Jr fly to Australia where Sinatra plays four concerts, all sell-outs. But Nancy becomes disillusioned with her father when she discovers in his room undies that belong to one of the show girls.

August 15-17

With Nelson Riddle, Frank records songs for the soundtrack of *Carousel* in which he is to play Billy Bigelow.

August 24

It's reported that Frank has walked out on the production of *Carousel* which is being made at Bootbay Harbor, Maine. He maintains that the picture is being shot in two processes, Todd-AO and CinemaScope and every scene has to be shot twice. "I do not intend to make two films at once," he protests. Gordon MacRae is quickly drafted in to take his place in the film. Ironically, the film is finally shot in one process only.

August 27

'Learning The Blues' climbs to No 2 in the UK singles chart and remains in that spot for five weeks, kept from the top by Slim Whitman's 'Rose Marie'.

September 3

Sinatra logs yet another UK hit single as 'Not As A Stranger' reaches No 18.

September 13

L.A. Frank records 'The Tender Trap' and 'You'll Get Yours' with Nelson Riddle.

September 19

NBC-TV screens the production of Thornton Wilder's *Our Town*, starring Sinatra, Paul Newman and Eva Marie Saint. Re-shaped as a musical, with a score by Sammy Cahn and Jimmy Van Heusen, it features the eventual hit 'Love And Marriage'.

October 17

Frank and Nelson Riddle record 'You Forgot All The Words', 'Weep They Will' and 'Love Is Here To Stay', the latter being the first track to be recorded for the 'Songs For Swingin' Lovers' album.

October 21

The film *The Tender Trap* is previewed. "It's a cute and capricious comedy, with the foursome of Sinatra, Debbie Reynolds, Celeste Holm and David Wayne often hitting the laughter mark. Sinatra must have liked the parade of gals that are chosen to decorate his existence before he falls victim to the tender trap – in the form of Miss Reynolds."

October 30

The state of Nevada approves a gambling licence for Sinatra, in spite of a protest by the State Tax Commission who aver that he should pay his back taxes first.

November 2

'Love And Marriage' enters the US charts and reaches No 5.

November 22

Deborah Kerr accompanies Frank to the Hollywood première of *Guys And Dolls*. A reviewer calls it "A Goldwyn Goldmine - a bangup film musical with Damon Runyan's story insured by a strong quartet in Marlon Brando, Jean Simmons, Frank Sinatra and Vivian Blaine and fortified by a good set of songs."

December

With 18 months to go on his original four-year deal, Frank signs a new seven-year contract with Capitol Records. Additionally, it's announced that he is to both produce and star in a Western that has the working title of *The Loud Law* but will eventually surface as *Johnny Concho*. Don McGuire is named as director and Keenan Wynn as co-star while Nelson Riddle is to contribute the score – his first-ever in a career that will see him provide the music to some 40 cinema and TV movies.

December 7

The film *The Man With The Golden Arm* is previewed. "This case history of a drug addict is gripping and fascinating film, directed by Otto Preminger and performed by Frank Sinatra as the drug slave."

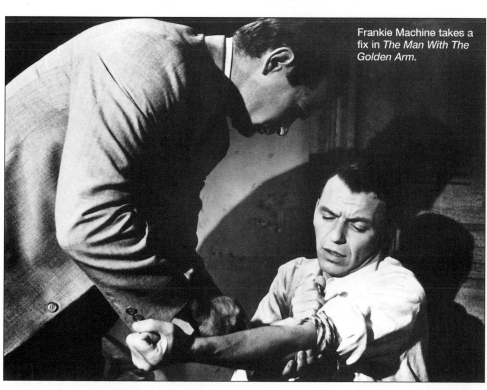

Frankie Machine takes a fix in *The Man With The Golden Arm*.

Frank with Phyllis Kirk in the movie *Johnny Concho.*

1956

January 9, 10, 12 & 16

At a series of landmark Los Angeles sessions with Nelson Riddle, Frank records 'You Brought A New Kind Of Love To Me', 'You Make Me Feel So Young', 'Pennies From Heaven', 'How About You', 'You're Getting To Be A Habit With Me', 'It Happened In Monterey', 'Swingin' Down The Lane', 'I've Got You Under My Skin', 'Makin' Whoopee', 'Old Devil Moon', 'Anything Goes', 'Too Marvellous For Words' and 'We'll Be Together Again', all of which will help form the 'Songs For Swingin' Lovers' album. Also on the same dates, such cuts as 'Memories Of You' and 'Flowers Mean Forgiveness' are pieced together.

January 21

'Love And Marriage' reaches No 3 in the UK singles chart.

February

Frank begins work on the film *High Society*, in which he co-stars with Bing Crosby, Grace Kelly, Celeste Holm and Louis Armstrong. A remake of *The Philadelphia Story*, a 1940 multi-Oscar winner, this version sports an engaging Cole Porter score. Grace Kelly had just become engaged to Prince Ranier of Monaco, who visited the set in Hollywood.

February 1

The film *Meet Me In Las Vegas*, starring Dan Dailey and Cyd Charisse is previewed. Sinatra makes a guest appearance, attempting to win on a fruit machine at the Sands Hotel.

February 11

The single '(Love Is) The Tender Trap' goes to No 3 in the UK charts, providing Frank with two records in the top five.

February 22 & 28

Frank once more takes up the baton to conduct an orchestral album called 'Tone Poems Of Colour'. Tracks: 'Black', 'Orange', 'White', 'Brown', 'Red' and 'Silver'. Elmer Bernstein, André Previn, Nelson Riddle and Victor Young are among the arrangers.

March 5

The 'Songs For Swingin' Lovers' LP is released in the US. The record, a 15-track affair, proves to be a classic, thanks in part to Nelson Riddle's memorable arrangements.

March 7

More work on the 'Tone Poems Of Colour' album, Frank conducting 'Yellow', 'Green', 'Grey' and 'Blue'.

March 8

Frank begins recording the 'Close To You' album with Nelson Riddle and the Hollywood String Quartet, cutting 'Don't Like Goodbyes', 'P.S. I Love You', 'Love Locked Out' and 'If It's The Last Thing I Do'.

March 15

The 'Tone Poems Of Colour' album is completed as Frank conducts 'Gold' and 'Purple', arranged by Nelson Riddle and Billy May respectively.

March 21

Sinatra is around to hand the Best Score award to Alfred Newman (*Love Is A Many Splendoured Thing*) at Hollywood's Oscar ceremony, but fails in his attempt to be named Best Actor for his role in *The Man With The Golden Arm*. Frank attends the ceremony in the company of singer-starlet Peggy Connolly.

April 4 & 5

The 'Close To You' sessions continue, as Frank lays down such tracks as 'I've Had My Moments', 'Blame It On My Youth', 'Everything Happens To Me', 'The End Of A Love Affair', 'With Every Breath I Take', also cutting 'Wait Till You See Her' and 'There's A Flaw In My Flue', a spoof ballad that everyone at Capitol takes seriously thanks to Frank's tongue-in-cheek delivery.

April 9

Los Angeles. With Nelson Riddle, Frank records 'Something Wonderful Happens In Summer', 'Five Hundred Guys', 'Hey Jealous Lover' and 'No One Ever Tells You'.

April 20

Los Angeles. The *High Society* soundtrack is pieced together, Frank recording 'You're Sensational', 'Mind If I Make Love To You' and 'Who Wants To Be A Millionaire', a duet with Celeste Holm.

Mr Supersmooth – Cary Grant.

Late April

In Spain, Frank begins work on the film *The Pride And The Passion*, based on C.S. Forester's book *The Gun*. Sophia Loren and Cary Grant are his co-stars and everyone seems miscast. But the gun itself – a dodgy cannon hauled halfway across Spain to help win a battle against Napoleon – proves likeable.

May 7

Los Angeles. The 'Well Did You Evah?' duet with Bing Crosby is recorded for High Society.

June 30

Though it's an album, 'Songs For Swingin' Lovers' sells so well that it climbs to No 12 in the UK singles chart!

July 1

Jack Bentley, in the *Sunday Pictorial*, reviews 'Swingin' Lovers' and advises the singer to 'watch out' and 'practise more'!

July 5

The film *Johnny Concho* is previewed in Hollywood. "For the first time, Frank draws both producer and star credits in this Western which inclines talkiness. In the title Frank plays the cowardly younger brother of a dreaded gunslinger." The release of *High Society* makes it two in a month for Sinatra, who fares well in this musical remake of *The Philadelphia Story*, which, despite a list of co-stars that includes Bing Crosby, Grace Kelly and Louis Armstrong, plus a score by Cole Porter, never really amounts to not much more than a pleasant romp.

July 28

Frank walks out on *The Pride And The Passion* and the film is finished without him.

July 31
In Rome, Ava Gardner announces that she and Frank have signed divorce papers.

August
Frank plays a week's engagement at the New York Paramount with The Dorsey Brothers band. The theatre is screening *Johnny Concho*.

September
Frank wins the inaugural Entertainer Of The Era Award presented by the Al Jolson Lodge of The B'Nai B'rith charity organisation at Hollywood's Coconut Grove.

October 1
The 'Close To You' sessions are completed as Frank records 'I Couldn't Sleep A Wink Last Night', 'It's Easy To Remember' and the album's title track.

October 16
Mike Todd's *Around The World In 80 Days* is previewed. An entertaining, monster-length (nearly three hours) adaptation of the Jules Verne classic, it allows Frank, one of the many star names in bit parts, to make a brief appearance as a piano player.

October 17
'Hey Jealous Lover' enters the US charts and reaches No 6.

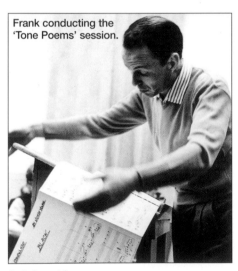

Frank conducting the 'Tone Poems' session.

October 19
The Rat Pack attend a dinner at Hollywood's Copa Room, those at the table include Humphrey Bogart, Judy Garland and David Niven.

November 15, 20, 26 & 28
The 'A Swingin' Affair' sessions take place in Los Angeles, Frank and Nelson Riddle recording: 'At Long Last Love', 'I Got Plenty Of Nuttin'', 'I Won't Dance', 'Stars Fell On Alabama', 'I Guess I'll Have To Change My Plan', 'I Wish I Were In Love Again', 'Nice Work If You Can Get It', 'Night And Day', 'The Lonesome Road', 'If I Had You', 'I Got It Bad And That Ain't Good', 'From This Moment On', 'Oh Look At Me Now', and 'You'd Be So Nice To Come Home To' plus 'The Lady Is A Tramp' which is omitted from the original album.

1957

January 14
Good friend Humphrey Bogart dies and Frank cancels his show at the Copacabana as a mark of respect.

January 21
'Close To You', an album of ballads in an almost chamber music setting is released in the US.

February
Frank and Doris Day are named music personalities of the year in *Downbeat* magazine's motion pictures awards.

February 4
Frank heads for Australia for a February 7 show in Sydney but the trip is terminated in Honolulu and the Oz concert is cancelled.

March 14
L.A. Frank records 'So Long My Love' and 'Crazy Love' with Nelson Riddle.

April 2, 4 & 8
Sinatra takes up the baton once more to conduct the orchestra on Peggy Lee's 'The Man I Love' album. Peg claims: 'The album was totally Frank's concept. He hired Nelson Riddle to write those lovely arrangements. He designed and supervised the cover, even putting menthol in my eyes so I'd have a misty look in the cover photograph."

April 10 & 29 and May 1
L.A. Frank and Gordon Jenkins record the 'Where Are You?' album. Tracks: 'Where Is The One?', 'There's No You', 'The Night We Called It A Day', 'Autumn Leaves', 'I Cover The Waterfront', 'Lonely Town', 'Laura', 'Baby, Won't You Please Come Home', 'Where Are You?', 'I Think Of You', 'I'm A Fool To Want You' and 'Maybe You'll Be There'.

May 6
'A Swingin' Affair', the sequel to 'Songs For Swingin' Lovers' is released in the US.

May 14
Look magazine publishes the first of three controversial articles on Sinatra, kicking off with one titled 'Talent, Tantrums And Torment'.

May 20
L.A. A Sinatra-Riddle session produces 'Witchcraft', 'Something Wonderful Happens In Summer', 'Tell Her You Love Her' and 'You're Cheatin' Yourself'.

June 9
Frank plays a concert with Nelson Riddle at Seattle's Civic Auditorium.

June 20
New York. The film *The Pride And The Passion* is previewed... "Locationed in Spain, Stanley Kubrick's powerful production of C.S. Forester's sweeping novel about a Spanish citizens' army that goes into battles against the conquering French legions in 1810, moves with excitement and suspense and has a provocative, highly attractive cast headed by Cary Grant, Frank Sinatra and Sophia Loren."

July 5
Frank and Ava finally get a divorce.

July 10, 16 & 17
It may be summer but Frank, Gordon Jenkins and The Ralph Brester Singers get together in L.A. to record 'A Jolly Christmas From Frank Sinatra'. Tracks: 'It Came Upon A Midnight Clear', 'O Little Town Of Bethlehem', 'Hark The Herald Angels Sing', 'Adeste Fideles', 'Jingle Bells', 'The First Noël', 'Have Yourself A Merry Little Christmas', 'The Christmas Waltz', 'Mistletoe And Holly', 'The Christmas Song', 'Silent Night' and 'I'll Be Home For Christmas'.

August 13
L.A. Frank and orchestra leader Morris Stoloff, using Nelson Riddle arrangements, record 'I Could Write A Book', 'There's A Small Hotel' and 'Bewitched' as part of the *Pal Joey* soundtrack. Also recorded is 'All The Way' and 'Chicago', both with Riddle.

Frank clowns it up in *The Joker Is Wild*.

August 23
The Joker Is Wild is previewed. Sinatra gives one of his most memorable onscreen

With Jeanne Crain in
The Joker Is Wild.

With Kim Novak in *Pal Joey*.

performances as nightclub performer Joe E Lewis and sings the film's theme 'All The Way'. "Frank is believable and forceful – alternatively sympathetic and pathetic, funny and sad."

September 1
'Can I Steal A Little Love' enters the US charts and reaches No 20.

September 25
L.A. Two additional *Pal Joey* songs are recorded 'I Didn't Know What Time It Was' and 'What Do I Care For A Dame?'

October 1, 3 & 8
L.A. The 'Come Fly With Me' album is recorded with Billy May. Tracks: 'On The Road To Mandalay', 'Let's Get Away From It All', 'Isle Of Capri', 'Autumn In New York', 'London By Night', 'April In Paris', 'Moonlight In Vermont', 'Blue Hawaii', 'Come Fly With Me', 'It's Nice To Go Trav'ling' and 'Brazil'.

October 26
'All The Way' enters the US singles chart and heads for No 15.

September 5
The film *Pal Joey* is previewed. "Frank is potent as the irreverent, free-wheeling, glib Joey in this racy (not for the kids and grandma) blockbuster from John O'Hara's original book. Standout of the score is 'The Lady Is A Tramp'. It's a wham arrangement and Sinatra gives it powerhouse delivery. Rita Hayworth moves with authority but Kim Novak is pallid."

October 13
The Edsel TV Show stars Frank, Bing Crosby, Lindsay Crosby, Louis Armstrong, Rosemary Clooney and The Four Preps.

October 18
Frank kicks off his ABC-TV series with a one-hour special, the guests being Peggy Lee, Bob

Hope and Kim Novak. The remainder of the series will consist of a mixture of half-hour musical programmes and some dramas, sponsored by various companies including Chesterfield cigarettes and Bulova watches. But they will lack viewing figures, leading to eventual cancellation of the series.

October 25
ABC-TV Sinatra appears in a drama titled *That Man Hogan*, with Jesse White.

October 30
In a *Daily Sketch* article, Frank writes: "I deplore this rancid, smelly aphrodisiac – rock'n'roll."

November 1
ABC-TV *Sinatra Show* – guest Nancy Sinatra.

November 4
Britain's Daily Herald reports that John Taylor, the editor of the *Tailor And Cutter* is 'dismayed and shattered' because the Custom Tailors' Guild have chosen President Eisenhower and Frank Sinatra to head their annual list of the 10 Best Dressed Men.

November 8
ABC-TV *Sinatra Show* – guest Peggy Lee.

November 15
ABC-TV *Sinatra Show* – guests The McGuire Sisters.

November 22
ABC-TV *Sinatra Show* – guest Erin O'Brien.

November 25
L.A. A session with Nelson Riddle produces 'Time After Time', 'I Believe', 'Everybody Loves Somebody' and 'It's The Same Old Dream'.

November 29
ABC-TV *Sinatra Show* – guest Dean Martin.

December 11
L.A. The final recording session of the year, with Nelson Riddle, produces 'You'll Always Be The One I Love', 'If You Are But A Dream' and 'Put Your Dreams Away', which together with the November 25 recordings will form part of the 'Look To Your Heart' album.

December 13
On ABC-TV Sinatra appears in a drama titled *Take Me To Hollywood*.

December 20
ABC-TV *Sinatra Show* – guest Bing Crosby.

December
In a *Metronome* magazine poll Frank is voted

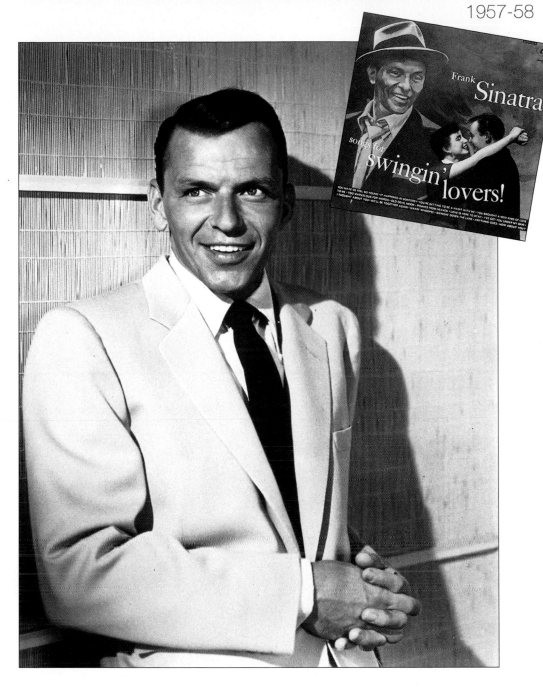

'Musicians' Musician Of The Year' by jazz performers, gaining more votes than all the other nominees combined.

December 28
'All The Way'/'Chicago' reaches No 5 in the UK singles chart. Both songs stem from the movie *The Joker Is Wild*.

1958

January 3
ABC-TV *Sinatra Show* – guest Dinah Shore.

January 6
US release of 'Come Fly With Me', an album on which Sinatra takes a musical world-trip, the often ebullient arrangements being by Billy May, once a trumpet star with Glenn Miller. The British version of the album, which doesn't arrive until September, differs from its American counterpart in that 'The Road To Mandalay' is omitted because of problems involving the Rudyard Kipling Estate, who object to Frank's hip updating ('a Burma broad is waitin'' etc.) of the Kipling poem.

January 10
ABC-TV *Sinatra Show* – guests Robert and Jim Mitchum.

January 17
ABC-TV *Sinatra Show* – guests Louis Prima and Keely Smith.

January 18
Club Oasis – *Sinatra TV Show* - guest Stan Freberg.

January 24
ABC-TV *Sinatra Show* – guest Jo Stafford.

January 25
'Witchcraft' enters the US charts and reaches No 20.

January 26
Frank guests on the Chevrolet-sponsored *Dinah Shore Show*.

January 31
ABC-TV *Sinatra Show* – guest Sammy Davis Jr.

February 1
Frank appears on NBC-TV's *Dean Martin Show*. Together, he and Dino take a shot at 'Jailhouse Rock'.

February
The UK release of 'Where Are You?' an album of songs about unrequited love. The ravishing string arrangements are by Gordon Jenkins, and an added incentive to buy is the fact that the recording is in stereo, marking Sinatra's first involvement in two-speaker technology, though initial British issues are in mono only.

February 7
ABC-TV *Sinatra Show* – guest Jeannie Carson.

February 14
ABC-TV *Sinatra Show* – guests Shirley Jones, Alice Pearce and Tina Sinatra.

February 28
ABC-TV *Sinatra Show* – guest Van Johnson.

March 1
'Witchcraft', an outstanding Carolyn Leigh-Cy Coleman song, reaches No 12 in the UK singles chart.

March 3
L.A. Frank records a brace of duets with Keely Smith, 'Nothing In Common' and 'How Are Ya Fixed For Love?', along with a solo 'Same Old Song And Dance'. Billy May is arranger.

March 7
ABC-TV *Sinatra Show* – guests Edie Adams and Stan Freberg.

March 11
Frank proposes to Lauren 'Betty' Bacall, Humphrey Bogart's widow. She accepts but the marriage never takes place.

March 14
ABC-TV *Sinatra Show* – guests Eydie Gorme and Joey Bishop.

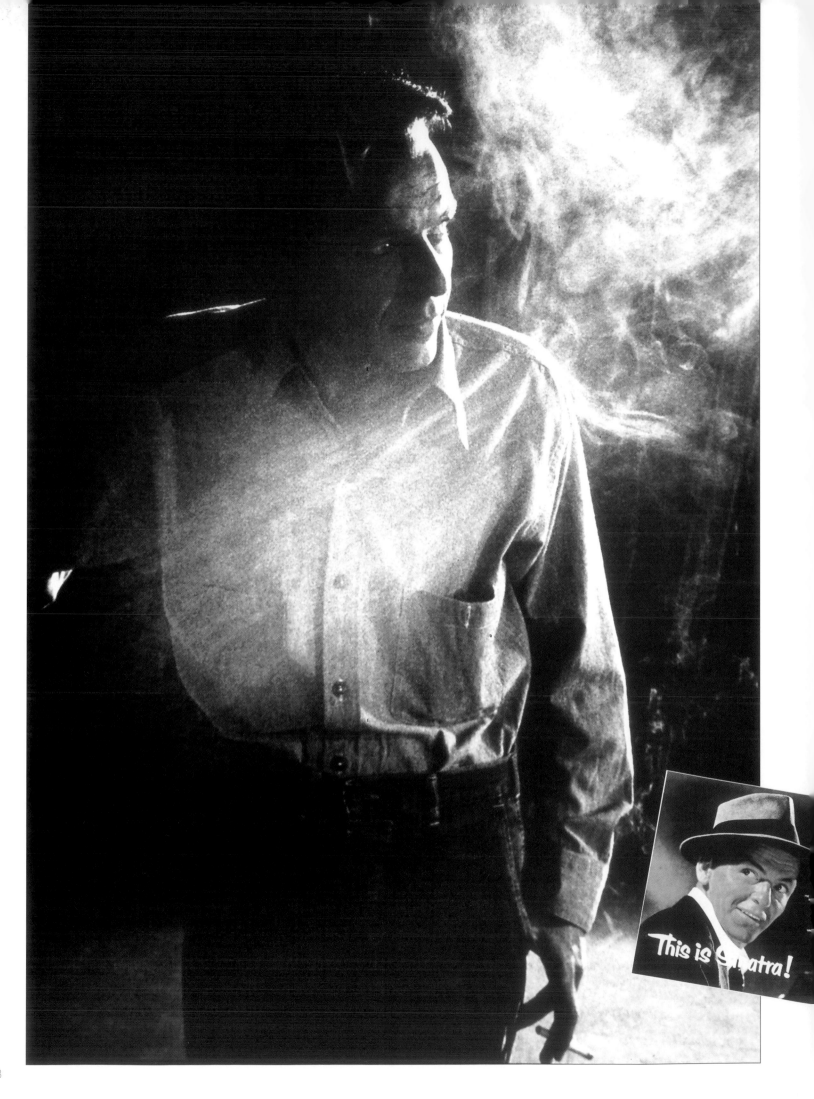

This is Sinatra!

March 21

A two-week appearance at the Fontainbleu, Miami, is concluded. During the stay Frank breaks every night club record in the book. "I am convinced that he is without doubt the greatest living vocal entertainer of the past 20 years," claims *NME*'s Maurice Kinn, who adds "The audience paid approximately £7 each!" However, one show is cancelled when Sinatra calls off due to a strained throat and the police take four hours to disperse the embittered crowd. Next night, the show is transferred to the hotel ballroom in order to accommodate the previous day's unlucky punters, though Frank describes the altered venue as being "like an aircraft hangar".

March 28

ABC-TV *Sinatra Show* – guests Spike Jones and Helen Greco.

April 8

Ella Fitzgerald guests on the *Sinatra Show*.

April 18

ABC-TV. Frank appears in the drama *The Brownstone Incident* with Cloris Leachman.

April 25

ABC-TV *Sinatra Show* – guest Ethel Merman.

May

Dean Martin hosts a SHARE children's charity party and Frank makes an appearance, embracing Sammy Davis Jr to show that they are friends once more. Together they sing 'The Lady Is A Tramp'.

May 9

ABC-TV *Frank Sinatra Show* – guest Ella Fitzgerald.

May 23

It's the final ABC-TV musical half-hour – guests Pat Suzuki and Natalie Wood.

May 29

L.A. At a marathon session Frank records 'Monique', a song from the the film *Kings Go Forth*, plus 'Ebb Tide', 'Angel Eyes', 'Spring Is Here', 'Guess I'll Have To Hang My Tears Out To Dry', 'Only The Lonely' and 'Willow Weep For Me', all of which will appear on the 'Only The Lonely' album. An attempt to record Billy Strayhorn's 'Lush Life' is also made but is never completed.

June 14

Sinatra takes a trip to Monte Carlo to attend the première of *Kings Go Forth*, a war movie in which he co-stars with Tony Curtis, the twosome portraying soldiers who fall for the same girl unaware that she's half-black. Following the screening, he plays a gala concert at the Monte Carlo Sporting Club and sings 'On The Road To Mandalay', commenting "Kipling's daughter had the nerve to ban that in England. How dare she? Still, she drinks a little bit, so we'll forgive her for that."

June 24/25

L.A. Frank completes the 'Only The Lonely' album, recording 'Blues In The Night', 'What's New?', 'Gone With The Wind', 'Goodbye', 'It's A Lonesome Old Town' and 'One For My Baby'.

July 7

It's reported that Frank has severed all sentimental links with Ava Gardner after having a statue of her as *The Barefoot Contessa* removed from the drive of his Hollywood home, where it has been for four years.

September 8

'Frank Sinatra Sings For Only The Lonely', a doomy but nevertheless compelling album of love-songs, arranged by Nelson Riddle, is released in the US. When, in the mid-Seventies, Sinatra is asked to name his favourite album, he chooses this one.

September 11

Los Angeles. With Nelson Riddle, Frank records 'Mr Success', 'Sleep Warm' and 'Where Or When'.

September 27

In London, Frank hosts the gala première of Danny Kaye's movie *Me And The Colonel*. Around £70,000 is raised for the British Cancer Fund at an event attended by the Queen and the Duke of Edinburgh.

September 30

Los Angeles. Frank and Billy May record 'It All Depends On You'.

Canoodling with Martha Hyer in *Some Came Running*.

October 1
A date with Nelson Riddle produces 'I Couldn't Care Less'.

October 13-15
Frank conducts on Dean Martin's 'Sleep Warm' album.

October 28 & December 5
Frank records 'To Love And Be Loved' with Nelson Riddle. Each session produces a different take and both are released.

December 9
The 'Come Dance With Me' LP sessions get underway as Frank records 'The Song Is You', 'Something's Gotta Give' and 'Just In Time' with Billy May.

December 15
Frank appears in the screen melodrama *Some Came Running*, as an ex-soldier who returns to a small mid-west town (actually Madison, Indiana) where disillusionment appears to be the main activity. Dean Martin, Martha Hyer and George Kennedy help out in this adaptation of James Jones' novel, but it's Shirley MacLaine as a good natured floozy, who grabs any plaudits that are going.

December 20
The single, 'Mr Success', reaches No 25 in the UK charts.

December 22/23
L.A. The 'Come Dance With Me' sessions are concluded, Frank recording 'Day In, Day Out', 'Baubles, Bangles And Beads', 'Dancing In The Dark', 'Saturday Night', 'Cheek To Cheek', 'Too Close For Comfort', 'I Could Have Danced All Night', 'Come Dance With Me' and 'The Last Dance'.

December 31
Frank attends a New Year's Eve dinner at Romanoff's with Robert Wagner, Natalie Wood, Peter Lawford and Lawford's wife, Pat Kennedy.

1959

January 26
The film *Some Came Running* opens in New York and is generally well-received. Directed by Vincente Minnelli and featuring a cast that links Sinatra, Dean Martin and Shirley MacLaine, it's an adaptation of James Joyce's novel about a disillusioned writer who returns to a

Frank with Dino in *Some Came Running*.

nowheresville small town and the company of a gambler (Martin) plus a prostitute (MacLaine).

January 28
At the Sands Hotel, Las Vegas, Sinatra and Dean Martin play their double-act for the very first time. *Variety* claims: "The pair put on one of the best shows ever seen at the Sands."

March 3
Billie Holiday, Frank's favourite singer, begins recording her 'Billie Holiday' album and tells arranger Ray Ellis that she wants a Sinatra sound, as she has been impressed by Gordon Jenkins' string charts for 'Only The Lonely'. The sessions feature such Sinatra-associated tracks as 'All The Way' and 'I'll Never Smile Again' and will be the last that Lady Day ever graces. That same night, Frank appears on *Some Of Manie's Friends*, an all-star TV tribute to Manie Sacks.

March 24, 25 & 26
L.A. Frank and Gordon Jenkins begin recording the 'No One Cares' album. Tracks: 'A Ghost Of A Chance', 'Why Try To Change Me Now?', 'None But The Lonely Heart', 'Stormy Weather', 'Here's That Rainy Day', 'I Can't Get Started', 'Where Do You Go?', 'A Cottage For Sale' and 'Just Friends' plus 'The One I Love Belongs To Somebody Else', which doesn't make it on to the original album.

April 1
Sinatra and the Red Norvo Quintet in concert at Australia's West Melbourne Stadium. While in the city, he stays with ex-wife Ava Gardner, who's there filming *On The Beach*, Nevil Shute's story about a world devasted by atomic warfare. At a show, he looks directly at her and sings 'All

of me, why not take all of me...' Later, Ava recalls, "With only two nights together, we didn't even have time to have a fight."

April 25
The single 'French Foreign Legion' reaches No 18 in the UK charts.

May 4
Frank attends the first Grammy Awards banquet at LA's Beverly Hilton Hotel and books two tables for himself and friends. But he loses out in category after category and fails to take home even a single award, though 'Only The Lonely' gets the Best Album cover plaudit.

May 8
L.A. Frank and Nelson Riddle record 'High Hopes' and 'Love Looks So Well On You'.

May 14
At two separate sessions Frank records 'This Was My Love' and 'Talk To Me' with Nelson Riddle, plus 'When No One Cares' and 'I'll Never Smile Again', completing the 'No One Cares' album. The comedy-drama *A Hole In The Head* gains a New York preview and Frank sings 'All My Tomorrows' over the film's credits, also putting in a convincing performance as a widower with a young son, who looks to his brother (Edward G. Robinson) a rich New York merchant, for financial assistance. Meanwhile, Frank's appearing on the SHARE Boomtown Show at Hollywood's Moulin Rouge, in the company of Dean Martin, Sammy Davis Jr., Jack Benny, Tony Curtis and a banjo-playing Kirk Douglas.

May 16
Frank places yet another album in the UK

Some Came Running.

Frank in *Never So Few.*

September 10

Frank hosts a Hollywood luncheon for visiting Russian Premier Nikita Krushchev and his wife Nina. Anti-Communist actor Ronald Reagan refuses to attend but Marilyn Monroe, Cary Grant, Eddie Fisher, Rita Hayworth and Gregory Peck are among those mixing the vodka and Californian wine. Krushchev visits the 20th Century Fox sound stage, where *Can Can* is being made. and Frank sings 'C'est Magnifique'. The Russian leader later labels the can-can dance sequence, performed by Juliet Prowse and Co., as "immoral".

singles chart as 'Come Dance With Me' climbs to No 30.

July 19

It's reported that Sinatra has received a minor eye injury while filming a battle scene in *Never So Few*, in Hollywood.

July 20

'No One Cares' yet another exhilarating album of songs to cut your wrists by, emerges in the States.

July 25

Frank plays an eight-day engagement at Atlantic City's 500 Club and so excites the fans that a reported two hundred women require treatment at the local hospital.

August

While making *Can Can* in Hollywood, Frank meets dancer Juliet Prowse and begins dating her.

August 16

The short feature film *Invitation To Monte Carlo* gains a London preview, Sinatra appearing in one scene.

The leggy Juliette Prowse.

September 27

An *Oldsmobile TV* special is screened, starring Sinatra, Peggy Lee, Bing Crosby, Louis Armstrong and Rosemary Clooney.

October

After Sinatra's car is dented in an L.A. collision, he chases the other motorist at high speed, broadcasting requests for help over his radio phone. The other driver, thinking Frank is a hold-up man, pulls into a police station and also requests aid.

October 19

WABC-TV present the first in a series of four one-hour Sinatra musical shows, sponsored by Timex. Guest stars Bing Crosby, Mitzi Gaynor and Dean Martin. Dean Martin and Bing Crosby guest on Frank's show, the trio singing 'Together'. It's announced that the threesome will soon be getting together to make a movie based on the life of Jimmy Durante. But the film will never be made.

November 7

The single 'High Hopes' which has been in the UK charts for some weeks, eventually reaches No 6.

November 29

Frank wins two Grammy Awards, the single 'Come Dance With Me' being adjudged Best Solo Vocal Performance, while the LP of that name gains the Album Of The Year plaudit.

December 2

The film *Never So Few* gets its first airing. It's an action-filled war romance, set in Burma, in which Frank, as a rugged, individualistic commander of a small British-American task force, leads a foray against a Japanese position near the Chinese border.

December 13

The second Timex Spectacular is aired. Titled *Frank Sinatra: An Afternoon With His Friends*, the friends prove to be Ella Fitzgerald, Hermione Gingold, Juliet Prowse, The Hi-Los and Peter Lawford, the last named being intent on promoting the Presidential ambitions of his brother-in-law, Senator John Kennedy.

December 28

One paper claims: "Frank Sinatra, who already has holdings in property, oil, a racetrack and sundry extra-entertainment, has now started an actors' agency. Presumably Mr Sinatra will now pay his agent's ten per cent to Mr Sinatra."

On the *Welcome Home Elvis* Show.

1960

February 15

The third Timex TV show is *Here's To The Ladies*, with Lena Horne, Juliet Prowse, Mary Costa, Barbara Heller and Mrs Eleanor Roosevelt.

February 19/20

Nelson Riddle arranges and conducts on sessions for the *Can Can* soundtrack album, the songs including 'It's All Right With Me', 'C'est

Magnifique', 'I Love Paris' (with Shirley MacLaine), 'Montmartre' and 'I Love Paris', the last two being duets with Maurice Chevalier.

March 1-3

In Los Angeles, Riddle and Sinatra piece together tracks for the 'Nice'n'Easy' album. The songs: 'You Go To My Head', 'Fools Rush In', 'That Old Feeling', 'Try A Little Tenderness', 'She's Funny That Way', 'Nevertheless', 'Dream', 'I've Got A Crush On You', 'Embraceable You', 'Mam'selle', 'How Deep Is The Ocean' and 'The Nearness Of You', though the last-named will end up on another album.

March

Elvis Presley is demobbed and films *Welcome Home Elvis*, a TV spectacular with Frank. Pre-recorded at the Fontainebleau in Miami, the

show features the twosome switching material, Elvis singing 'Witchcraft' and Sinatra tackling 'Love Me Tender'.

March 6

Radio Luxembourg begins a new series of record programmes called *The Magic Of Sinatra*.

March 12

The highly publicised *Can Can* is released. "This serviceable musical has Cole Porter songs but lacks stature. The juxtaposition of Sinatra and Shirley MacLaine on one hand, and authentic Parisians Maurice Chevalier and Louis Jourdan on the other, just doesn't work."

March 21

Frank's intention of employing scriptwriter

The Clan in *Oceans Eleven*.

confirmed that John Kennedy has received enough to ensure his nomination as Democratic candidate for the Presidency. That same day it's announced in Carson City that Sinatra, Dean Martin, plus friends Hank Sanicola and Skinny D'Amato, have applied to take over a majority interest in the Cal-Neva Lodge.

July 25
US release of 'Nice'n'Easy', an album that lives up to its name via a warm, armchair approach, being neither punchy nor particularly poignant.

August 3
The movie *Oceans Eleven* receives its world première. The film stars The Clan, Frank, and a group of friends that includes Dean Martin, Sammy Davis Jr, Peter Lawford and Joey Bishop. The storyline about a group of ex-Army buddies who raid five Las Vegas casinos proves a winner and the film pulls in big bucks at the box-office.

August 22 & 23
In Los Angeles, Frank and Nelson Riddle record 'When You're Smiling', 'I Concentrate On You', 'You Do Something To Me', 'S'posin'', 'Should I?', 'My Blue Heaven', 'I Can't Believe That You're In Love With Me', 'Always' and 'It All Depends On You'.

August 31 & September 1
Sinatra and Riddle conclude the 'Sinatra's Swingin' Session' dates by recording 'It's Only A Paper Moon' and 'September In The Rain' and 'Blue Moon' along with 'Hidden Persuasion', 'Ol' MacDonald' and 'Sentimental Baby'.

September 11
Daughter Nancy marries actor/pop star Tommy Sands at The Sands, Las Vegas. Among the guests are Joe DiMaggio and songwriter Jimmy Van Heusen. Soon after the ceremony, Sands, an Air Force reservist, returns to his base at Long Beach.

September 13
The Nevada Gaming Control Board recommend the Cal-Neva takeover for approval.

October 8
The single 'Nice'n'Easy' reaches No 18 in the UK charts.

November 1
Sinatra guests on NBC-TV's *The Dean Martin Show*, along with comedian Don Knotts and actress-singer Dorothy Provine. The show is based around the question "will Sinatra take time off from filming *The Devil At Four O'Clock*"? He does and provides the show's highspot in a hits medley with Martin.

Albert Maltz to provide the screenplay for a film, backfires. The film is to be based on a controversial book *The Execution Of Private Slovak* by William Bradford Huie and deals with the story of the only American soldier to be executed since the Civil War era. The choice of Maltz stirs further problems because the writer once declined to testify before the Un-American Activities Committee regarding alleged membership of the Communist Party. With virtually the whole of Hollywood ganging up on him, including his friends, Sinatra is forced to drop both Maltz and the picture.

March 23
Work is completed on the movie *Oceans Eleven*.

April 12
With Nelson Riddle, Frank records 'Nice'n'Easy', 'River Stay 'Way From My Door', 'I Love Paris' and 'It's Over, It's Over, It's Over'.

May 12
The fourth Sinatra Timex show, *Welcome Home Elvis*, is networked, achieving the highest viewing figures for any TV show in five years.

May 13
Hollywood. Frank dines with Juliet Prowse at a celebrity dinner.

June 25
A single featuring Frank's version of 'River Stay 'Way From My Door', a song penned in 1931, reaches No 16 in the UK charts.

July 10
Frank attends the Democratic National Convention in Los Angeles and backs John Kennedy. A $100 a plate fund-raising dinner is held at the Beverly Hilton Hotel, attended by 2,800 guests, including Sinatra and such fellow stars as Judy Garland, Peter Lawford, Angie Dickinson, Janet Leigh and Tony Curtis.

July 11
Frank sings 'The Star Spangled Banner' at the opening of the Democrats convention at the local sports arena – but delegates from Mississippi boo Sammy Davis Jr.

July 13
Frank is at the Convention Hall when it's

November 6 & 7
A Presidential visit enables Frank to place a plaque on a bedroom door at his Palm Springs home that reads: "John F. Kennedy Slept Here, November 6th and 7th, 1960."

November 8
It's Presidential election day and Frank stays in his L.A. office of Essex Productions checking incoming results and crossing his fingers on Kennedy's behalf.

November 9
At 3.10 in the morning, Nixon appears on TV but refuses to concede defeat because the voting is close. Frank, still watching and waiting, attempts to phone Nixon to tell him to get it over with.

November 13
Sammy Davis Jr marries Mai Britt in a Jewish ceremony held at his Hollywood home. Frank is best man. Realising that the mixed marriage will raise criticism from bigots, Sinatra maintains: "We're all behind Sam – if ever a guy deserved happiness, he does."

December 12
The Film Exhibitors of America vote Frank Top Box Office Star of 1960.

December 19
The film *Pepe* reaches cinema screens. Sinatra has a cameo role playing a scene in which he teaches Cantiflas how to gamble, Las Vegas style.

December 19/20
The first sessions for Sinatra's own label are recorded. Johnny Mandel supplies the arrangements as Frank sings 'Ring-A-Ding-Ding', 'Let's Fall In Love', 'In The Still Of The Night', 'A Foggy Day', 'Let's Face The Music And Dance', 'You'd Be So Easy To Love', 'A Fine Romance', 'The Coffee Song', 'Be Careful It's My Heart', 'I've Got My Love To Keep Me Warm', 'You And The Night And The Music', 'When I Take My Sugar To Tea', 'Have You Met Miss Jones?' and 'Zing Went The Strings Of My Heart'. The first twelve songs are to form the 'Ring-A-Ding-Ding' LP but 'Zing' is lost for many years, though it will later be discovered and placed on the CD version of the album.

December 21
Another own label session, this time with Felix Slatkin supplying the back-ups. The songs – 'The Last Dance', 'The Second Time Around' and 'Tina', the last-named being penned in honour of Frank's younger daughter.

1961

January 1
Frank launches his own label, Reprise Records.

January 19
Sinatra produces a Presidential Inaugural Gala at Washington's National Guard Armoury, the guest list including Gene Kelly, Peter Lawford, Juliet Prowse, Mahalia Jackson, Harry Belafonte, Anthony Quinn, Ethel Merman, Nat Cole, Shirley MacLaine, Ella Fitzgerald, Sir Laurence Olivier, Louis Prima, Leonard Bernstein, Bette Davis and Jimmy Durante, while Ella Fitzgerald is persuaded to fly in from Australia for just five minutes. The show is recorded and pressed as a double-album. But copies are only given to performers involved in the event. The event raises over a million and a half dollars to help out the depleted coffers of the Democratic Party, which were over four million down following the election campaign.

January 26
As Reprise Records readies its initial releases, Joseph Csida, president of Capitol Records says: "We wish Frank all the luck in the world. Because, frankly, he will need it."

Bill 'Count' Basie.

January 27
New York. Carnegie Hall. Frank, and friends that include Count Basie, Tony Bennett and Mahalia Jackson stage a tribute to Martin Luther King, who has just been released from a Georgia jail.

February 25
Frank and Dean Martin guest on *The Judy Garland Show*.

March 20, 21 & 22
Los Angeles. Frank gets together with Billy May to record 'On The Sunny Side Of The Street', 'Day By Day', 'Sentimental Journey', 'Don't Take

Your Love From Me', 'Yes Indeed', 'That Old Black Magic', 'Five Minutes More', 'I've Heard That Song Before', 'American Beauty Rose', 'Almost Like Being In Love', 'Lover' and 'Paper Doll' for the 'Come Swing With Me' album.

March 29
Louella Parsons reports "the whole town is buzzing about Frank Sinatra's lavish gifts to ex-wife Nancy on her birthday – a $10,000 mink coat and a diamond watch".

April
'Ring-A-Ding-Ding', Frank's début album for Reprise Records is released.

April 12
At the third Grammy Awards shindig, 'Can Can' is adjudged the best soundtrack album of the year.

May 1-3
Frank works with ex-Dorsey arranger Sy Oliver on the 'I Remember Tommy' album, recording 'I'll Be Seeing You', 'I'm Getting Sentimental Over You', 'Imagination', 'Take Me', 'Without A Song', 'Polka Dots And Moonbeams', 'Daybreak', 'The One I Love Belongs To Somebody Else', 'There Are Such Things', 'It's Always You', 'It Started All Over Again' and 'East Of The Sun'.

May 17
A recording session with Billy May results in four unreleased takes.

May 18, 19 & 23
Frank records the 'Sinatra Swings' album with Billy May. The songs: 'The Curse Of An Aching Heart', 'Love Walked In', 'Please Don't Talk About Me When I'm Gone', 'Have You Met Miss Jones?', 'Don't Be That Way', 'I Never Knew', 'Falling In Love With Love', 'It's A Wonderful World', 'Don't Cry Joe', 'You're Nobody Till Somebody Loves You', 'Moonlight On The Ganges' and 'Granada'.

July 10
The Democratic Convention is held at the Beverly Hills Hotel. Sinatra and Sammy Davis Jr., Judy Garland, Mort Sahl, Joe E. Lewis are among the many entertainers who help fill the hotel's two ballrooms. Frank later sits on the dais with John Kennedy, Lyndon Johnson, Adlai Stevenson and Eleanor Roosevelt.

July 26
The Rat Pack – Sinatra, Dean Martin, Sammy Davis Jr. and Joey Bishop – break up Eddie Fisher's opening at a Hollywood night club, and give an impromptu show. Fisher sits disconsolately nearby but later claims that he enjoyed it all.

August

In Los Angeles Supreme Court, Capitol Records is granted a temporary injunction restraining Reprise from selling Sinatra's 'Swing Along With Me' album, claiming that the title is too similar to Capitol's 'Come Swing With Me'. Reprise accordingly rush-release the LP under the title 'Sinatra Swings'.

August 5

Frank and Dean Martin fly into London to make guest appearances in the Crosby and Hope movie *The Road To Hong Kong*.

September 11

British writer Robin Douglas Home flies to L.A. at Frank's invitation to attend a recording session for the 'Point Of No Return' album. Later, he's invited to stay with Sinatra and remains constantly in the singer's company for two months, this encounter resulting in a book *This Is Sinatra*, which will be published by Michael Joseph in 1962. On the first day of the session, Sinatra, reunited with Axel Stordahl for what will be his final Capitol album, records 'I'll Be Seeing You', 'I'll See You Again', 'September Song', 'Memories Of You', 'There Will Never Be Another You' and 'When The World Was Young'.

September 12

The sessions with Stordahl are completed, the songs taped being 'Somewhere Along The Way', 'A Million Dreams Ago', 'These Foolish Things', 'As Time Goes By', 'It's A Blue World' and 'I'll Remember April'.

September 20

Reprise makes its bow in Britain through a deal with Pye Records, providing UK punters with access to new material not only by Frank but also by Nancy Sinatra, Mort Sahl, Ben Webster, Tony Williams, Mavis Rivers, Jimmy Witherspoon and others. It's announced that, from October 5, DJ Kent Walton will present *The Reprise Show* on Radio Luxembourg.

September 24

Frank is a guest at President Kennedy's Hyannis Port home. He flies in on the President's personal plane though the Hyannis airport is closed, due to fog, and he and his party have to de-plane at New Bedford and catch a taxi to complete their trip.

October 7

The single 'Granada' reaches No 11 in the UK charts.

October 12

The film *The Devil At 4 O'Clock* is released. "It's an exciting tropical island adventure yarn in which priest Spencer Tracy and convict Frank Sinatra save the lives of children in a leper hospital after a volcano erupts."

November 4

Sammy Davis Jr. is completing his show at the Sands, Las Vegas, when Sinatra joins him onstage. Davis eventually being carried off for over-running on his act and "stopping the customers gambling".

November 5

Sinatra rehearses at 2.30 am for a his two-week stay at the Sands. In the evening, his performance, backed by the Antonio Morelli Orchestra, is recorded. But the projected live album is never released.

November 20-22

Recording sessions with Don Costa. The songs: 'As You Desire Me', 'Stardust', 'Yesterday', 'I Hadn't Anyone Till You', 'It Might As Well Be Spring', 'Prisoner Of Love', 'That's All', 'Don't Take Your Love From Me', 'Misty', 'Come Rain Or Come Shine', 'Night And Day', 'All Or Nothing At All'.

November 22

At a session with Nelson Riddle, Frank records 'Pocketful Of Miracles' and 'Name It And It's Yours'.

December 2

A date at Sydney Stadium, the final show in a three-concert Australian jaunt.

1962

January 9

The news breaks that Frank has become engaged to leggy South African dancer Juliet Prowse (once a chorus girl at the London Palladium and a former girlfriend of Elvis Presley) who appeared in *Can Can* with Sinatra.

January 15

Frank records 'All Alone', an album of waltzes with Gordon Jenkins. Songs: 'The Song Is Ended', 'All Alone', 'Charmaine', 'When I Lost You', 'Remember', 'Together', 'The Girl Next Door', 'Indiscreet', 'What'll I Do?', 'Oh How I Miss You Tonight' and 'Are You Lonesome Tonight'. The intended title track 'Come Waltz With Me' is recorded but not used.

February 10

Sergeants 3 is released, the film is described as "warmed-over Gunga Din in which a summit meeting of Clan members is convened. Sinatra, Dean Martin and Peter Lawford re-enacting the roles played in the original by Cary Grant, Victor McLaglen and Douglas Fairbanks Jr."

February 17

Philadelphia radio station WING decides that it's 'Frank Sinatra Day' and regales its listeners with a virtually non-stop diet of Sinatra songs.

February 22

Six weeks in the wake of Frank's engagement to Juliet Prowse comes the news that the liaison has been terminated due to a "conflict of career interests".

February 25

The Judy Garland Show, with Frank and Dean Martin guesting, is aired over NBC, Sinatra setting the tone when he sings to Judy: "You're much too marvellous, too marvellous for words."

Woody Herman.

February 27

With Woody Herman/Count Basie arranger Neal Hefti, Frank records 'Everybody's Twistin'' and 'Nothing But The Best'.

March 5

The US release of 'Point Of No Return', the album that concludes Sinatra's contract with Capitol Records. A ballad offering, it reunites Sinatra with Axel Stordahl, the very arranger with whom Frank had first recorded for the label.

March 23

The Road To Hong Kong is released and stars Bob Hope and Bing Crosby who discover spacemen/guest artists Frank Sinatra and Dean Martin as they land on the planet Plutonius.

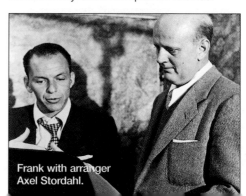
Frank with arranger Axel Stordahl.

April 10 & 11
At a two-day Hollywood session Frank records 'I'm Beginning To See The Light', 'I Get A Kick Out Of You', 'Ain't She Sweet', 'I Love You', 'They Can't Take That Away From Me', 'Love Is Just Around The Corner', 'At Long Last Love', 'Serenade In Blue', 'Goody, Goody', 'Doncha Go Way Mad', 'Tangerine' and 'Pick Yourself Up'. The arranger is Neal Hefti.

April 15
Sinatra plays a date in Mexico City as he sets out on tour to raise a million dollars for children's charities, a round-the-world affair that will encompass stop-overs in Tokyo, Hong Kong, Tel Aviv, Athens, Rome, Milan, Paris, Monte Carlo, London and New York. The accompanying sextet includes Bill Miller (piano), Harry Klee (reeds), Al Viola (guitar), Ralph Pena (bass) and Irv Cottler (drums). The tour is to be filmed for a TV spectacular with all proceeds going to under-privileged American children. The cost of the tour will be borne by Frank himself.

April 20 & 21
Concerts in Tokyo.

April 21
In a chart dominated by such records as Sam Cooke's 'Twistin' The Night Away' plus Chubby Checker's 'Let's Twist Again' and 'Slow Twistin'', Frank's 'Everybody's Twistin' just creeps into the UK Top 30.

April 26-28
Concerts in Hong Kong.

May 15-22
Frank takes a break from touring and embarks on a cruise around the Eastern Mediterranean.

May 24
A concert in Rome.

May 25
More Italian concerts, this time in Milan.

June 1
Midnight. Sinatra appears at London's Royal Festival Hall for the first concert of his British tour. Hundreds of jostling people attempt to gatecrash the show and organisers describe the trouble as the worst ever seen at the hall. The show lasts three hours and Frank is onstage for 105 minutes, with only one break. Touts offer tickets at ten times their face value and proceeds are estimated at £30,000 for British charities. There are no freebie tickets and even Sinatra foots the bill for tickets for his guests. In the States, the Otto Preminger-directed *Advise And Consent*, Charles Laughton's last movie, is released. Frank supplies the film's theme song.

Frank in London with arranger Nelson Riddle (left) and bandleader Vic Lewis (centre)

June 2
The Odeon, Leicester Square.

June 3
Two concerts at The Gaumont, Hammersmith.

June 5
A live show in Paris, introduced by Charles Aznavour, is recorded but will remain unreleased on album until 1994. Guitarist Al Viola later comments: "At the beginning of the tour we were sluggish. The first gig in Mexico City was the first time we'd worked with Frank (as a unit). But as we went along to Tokyo, Rome, Athens, Tel Aviv and so on we developed our own shadings. By the time we got to Paris we were locked in."

June 6
The Midnight Matinee show of June 1 is screened in the UK on ABC TV.

June 12-14
Sinatra records his only made-in-Britain album with Canadian arranger-bandleader Bob Farnon. Recorded live before a small audience of friends and admirers at a London Bayswater studio, it is titled 'Great Songs From Great Britain' and features such songs as 'If I Had You', 'The Very Thought Of You', 'I'll Follow My Secret Heart', 'A Garden In The Rain', 'London By Night', 'The Gypsy', 'A Nightingale Sang In Berkeley Square', 'We'll Meet Again', 'Now Is The Hour' and 'We'll Gather Lilacs'. The singer rejects a record company 'bright idea' to place a portrait of Sir Winston Churchill on the sleeve. The album will remain unreleased in the US until 1993.

June 15
Princess Alexandra visits Frank at the Savoy Hotel. Later, Sinatra, Eddie Fisher and friends board a coach to go to a London cinema for a sneak preview of *The Manchurian Candidate.*

June 17
Frank plays a concert in Monte Carlo. It's the last date on his world tour.

June 18
Sinatra returns to the States, having completed his around-the-world charity tour. Later, asked what particular incident stood out in his mind, Sinatra replies "The moment I'll never forget is when I was visiting a home for blind kids in London and one little girl came up to me and asked: "What colour is the wind?" I didn't know what to answer, so in the end, I just said: "Nobody knows because the wind moves too fast"."

June 30
At Frank's Cal-Neva Lodge, on the California-Nevada border, Sinatra gets into a fight with Deputy-Sheriff Richard E. Anderson, who has married one of Frank's girlfriends. In the ensuing bust-up, Frank gets hit so hard that he's unable to perform for some days afterwards.

July 11
Frank opens his first business venture in northern Nevada, the remodelled Cal-Neva Lodge. Sinatra himself tops the bill.

August 3
Bobby Kennedy receives a formal report on Sinatra. It's nineteen single-spaced pages long and goes into detail regarding Frank's contacts with various gangsters. But all the 'evidence' they possess is a phone tape in which mobster Sam Giancana boasts that he owns a percentage of Cal-Neva Lodge.

August 25
Frank plays the 500 Club, Atlantic City, with Dean Martin and Sammy Davis Jr.

August 27
Los Angeles. Neal Hefti conducts, but the arrangements are by Nelson Riddle as Frank records 'The Look Of Love' and 'I Left My Heart In San Francisco' but the single is withdrawn just two weeks after US release.

September 26
Frank, along with his records and films, is banned from all Arab countries by the Arab League who accuse him of conducting Israeli propaganda.

October 2 & 3
Los Angeles. Neal Hefti provides the arrangements as Sinatra and The Count Basie Orchestra record an album for Reprise. Songs: 'Nice Work If You Can Get It', 'Please Be Kind', 'I Won't Dance', 'Learnin' The Blues', 'I'm Gonna Sit Right Down And Write Myself A Letter', 'I Only Have Eyes For You', 'My Kind Of Girl', 'Pennies From Heaven', 'The Tender Trap and 'Looking At The World Through Rose Coloured Glasses'.

October
A landslide nearly removes the foundations of Frank's bungalow in Coldwater Canyon, Beverly Hills.

October 22
Frank and Sammy Davis Jr record a Billy May arrangement of 'Me And My Shadow' in Los Angeles.

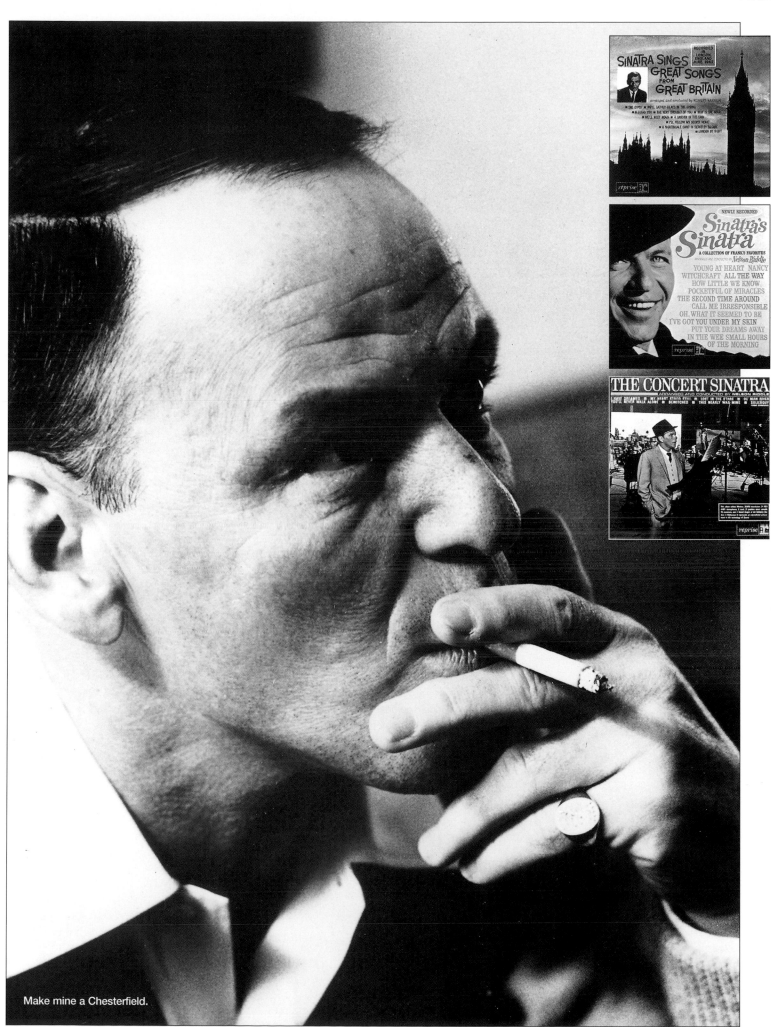

Make mine a Chesterfield.

47

October 24

The Manchurian Candidate is released. The film is based on Richard Condon's novel about a brainwashed Korean war hero who's being used by his mother and others in order to promote the career of a McCarthy-like politician. Sinatra lines up alongside Laurence Harvey, Janet Leigh and Angela Lansbury to create one of the year's most potent thrillers.

October 30

Frank and Ava attend an Adlai Stevenson rally in Hollywood.

December 12

Frank appears on TV's *Dinah Shore Show*, along with a cast that includes The Gerry Mulligan Quartet.

December 29

Frank's 'Me And My Shadow' duet with Sammy Davis Jr. reaches No 19 in the UK singles chart.

1963

January 21

Los Angeles. At a reunion with Nelson Riddle, Frank cuts a single 'Come Blow Your Horn' and 'Call Me Irresponsible'.

February 10

In New Jersey, Marty and Dolly Sinatra celebrate their fiftieth wedding anniversary with Frank and the whole family in attendance.

February 18, 19, 20 & 21

Hollywood. Frank and Nelson Riddle record 'Lost In The Stars', 'My Heart Stood Still', 'Ol' Man River', 'This Nearly Was Mine', 'You'll Never Walk Alone', 'I Have Dreamed', 'Bewitched', 'Soliloquy' and 'You Brought A New Kind Of Love To Me' along with unissued versions of 'California' and 'America The Beautiful'.

April 7

Frank puts his private plane up for sale priced at £100,000. It boasts its own grand piano, its own bar and a number of luxurious couches and chairs.

April 8

At the Oscar ceremony, live from Santa Monica Auditorium, Sinatra welcomes "the greatest pizza maker in the world – Sophia Loren" and presents the award for the Best Song.

April 30

Los Angeles. It's album time again as Frank and

Nelson Riddle record new versions of 'In The Wee Small Hours Of The Morning', 'Nancy', 'Young At Heart', 'The Second Time Around', 'All The Way', 'Witchcraft', 'How Little We Know', 'Put Your Dreams Away', 'I've Got You Under My Skin' and 'Oh What It Seemed To Be'.

May 29

The film *The List Of Adrian Messenger* is released. "It's a bizarre murder mystery about a British Intelligence Officer's efforts to catch a killer who had murdered eleven people, all heirs to a huge fortune." Frank briefly appears in the film – in disguise!

June 5

Sinatra appears as the playboy bachelor and Tony Bill as the hero-worshipping younger brother, in the film adaptation of Neil Simon's Broadway play *Come Blow Your Horn*.

July 10

Los Angeles. A session with Dean Martin and Sammy Davis Jr. produces a version of 'We Open In Venice'. Additionally Frank cuts 'Guys And Dolls' with Dean.

July 17

Chicago gang boss Sam Giancana moves into chalet No 50 at Cal-Neva, in which his wife, singer Phyllis McGuire, stays when appearing at the hotel. Giancana, as usual, is under FBI surveillance.

July 18

Los Angeles. Sinatra, conductor Morris Stoloff and arranger Nelson Riddle record 'Old Devil Moon', 'When I'm Not Near The Girl I Love' and 'I've Never Been In Love Before'.

July 24

Los Angeles. Frank records 'So In Love', with Keely Smith, 'Guys And Dolls (Reprise)' with Dean Martin, 'Some Enchanted Evening' with Rosemary Clooney and a solo version of 'Luck Be A Lady'.

July 27

At Lake Tahoe, FBI agents, continuing their investigations regarding alleged Mafia connections, photograph Frank playing golf with Sam Giancana.

July 29

A recording date with Bing Crosby and Dean Martin produces 'Fugue For Tinhorns' and 'The Oldest Established (Permanent Floating Crap Game In New York)'.

July 31

At a Los Angeles recording date, Frank cuts 'Some Enchanted Evening', 'Twin Soliloquies (I Wonder How It Feels?)', 'Here's To Losers' and 'Love Isn't Just For The Young'.

August

Reprise Records merges with Warner Bros, with Frank receiving a cheque for one million dollars but still retaining one third ownership of the label.

August 30

Old friend and long-time arranger Axel Stordhal dies, age 50.

September 13

Frank plays a show at the United Nations Building in New York, with Skitch Henderson at the piano

October 5 & 6

Frank lines up alongside Lena Horne for charity concerts at Carnegie Hall.

October 8

It's announced that Sinatra is to give up his Nevada gaming interests, reckoned to be worth £1,250,000.

October 13

Los Angeles. Frank records 'Have Yourself A Merry Little Christmas' with orchestra-leader Gus Levene and a chorus.

November 22

President John Kennedy is assassinated in Dallas, Texas.

December 3

Los Angeles. A recording date with Don Costa results in 'Talk To Me Baby' and 'Stay With Me'.

December 8

Frank Jr. is kidnapped at gunpoint at Lake Tahoe's Harrah's Casino, where he is about to perform. The kidnappers then contact Frank who agrees to a ransom of $240,000 which is dropped in an agreed location. Later, a blindfolded Frank Jr. is discovered nearly 500 miles away, in Bel-Air, L.A. That same night NBC screen *The Best On Records*, a show about the Grammy Awards. Sponsored by Timex, the show is only aired by NBC after Sinatra, Bing Crosby and Bob Hope agree to appear, Sinatra having been contacted by George Simon, the former jazz critic who provided Sinatra's first rave review of any importance. Originally

Sinatra directs *None But The Brave.*

scheduled for November 24, the show is put back to December following the assassination of President Kennedy.

December 15
Sinatra and Dean Martin perform at The Sands.

December 18
The film *Four For Texas* is released. "In this Western, which is too occupied with sex and romance, Frank and Dean Martin play two feuding soldiers of fortune who eventually have to join forces in vanquishing the threat of their mutual enemies, a treacherous banker (Victor Buono) and a hapless gunslinger (Charles Bronson)."

December 19
The World War II movie *The Victors* is released. A key scene features deserters being shot as Frank croons 'Have Yourself A Merry Little Christmas' on the soundtrack.

1964

January 2
Los Angeles. Frank, with Fred Waring and His Pennsylvanians begin recording a patriotic album called 'America I Hear You Singing'. Tracks laid down – 'You're A Lucky Fellow Mr Smith', 'The House I Live In' and 'Early American'.

January 22
At the Sands the billing reads 'Dean Martin & Friend'. The friend is Sinatra and the twosome have their own bar cart onstage.

January 27 & 28
Los Angeles. Frank and Nelson Riddle record the 'Academy Award Winners' album cutting such tracks as 'The Way You Look Tonight', 'Three Coins In The Fountain', 'Swinging On A Star', 'In The Cool, Cool, Cool Of The Evening', 'The Continental', 'It Might As Well Be Spring', 'Secret Love', 'Moon River', 'Love Is A Many Splendoured Thing' and 'Days Of Wine And Roses'.

February 4
Los Angeles. With Bing Crosby, Frank records 'Let Us Break Bread Together' and 'You Never Had It So Good'.

February 15
Frank guests on TV's *Bing Crosby Show*.

February
In Tokyo, work begins on *None But The Brave*, the film with which Frank will make his début as a movie director.

April 8
Los Angeles. With Nelson Riddle, Frank records 'My Kind Of Town', 'I Like To Lead When I Dance', additionally cutting 'I Can't Believe I'm Losing You' with Don Costa.

April 10
Sinatra, Bing Crosby, Dean Martin and Sammy Davis Jr. record three songs for the *Robin And The Seven Hoods* soundtrack album – 'Style', 'Mister Booze' and 'Don't Be A Do-Badder'.

April 13
Once more Sinatra's onstage at the annual Academy Awards shindig, this time presenting the plaudit given for Best Picture to David Picker of United Artists for *Tom Jones*.

May 2
The William Holden-Audrey Hepburn movie *Paris When It Sizzles* opens in New York. Nelson Riddle provides the score, Frank sings 'The Girl Who Stole The Eiffel Tower' and appears in a party scene.

May 10
It's reported that Frank is nearly drowned off the shores of Kauai, where's he's filming *None But The Brave*. Swamped by giant waves, he's rescued by actor Brad Dexter but requires the kiss of life.

June 9, 10 & 12
In Los Angeles Frank gets together with The Count Basie band and arranger Quincy Jones to record 'The Best Is Yet To Come', 'I Wanna Be Around', 'I Believe In You', 'Fly Me To The Moon', 'Hello Dolly', 'The Good Life', 'I Wish You Love', 'I Can't Stop Loving You', 'More' and 'Wives And Lovers' for the 'It Might As Well Be Swing' album.

June 16
Los Angeles. Frank records 'An Old Fashioned Christmas', 'I Heard The Bells On Christmas Day' and 'The Little Drummer Boy' with Fred Waring and His Pennsylvanians.

June 19
Los Angeles. Bing Crosby joins Sinatra and Waring to record 'Go Tell It On The Mountain' and 'We Wish You The Merriest'.

June 24
Robin And The Seven Hoods is released. The movie is a gangster spoof set in the Prohibition era, with Bing Crosby joining all the Clan regulars in a fight against such baddies as Guy Gisborne (Peter Falk) and Sheriff Potts (Victor Buono). The score includes the Sinatra hit 'My Kind Of Town'.

Robin And The Seven Hoods.

June 28
Frank guests on *The Ed Sullivan Show* and airs 'My Kind Of Town'.

July 11
There's a trip to Israel, where a Tel Aviv youth centre, for both Jews and Arabs, is named in Frank's honour.

July 17
Los Angeles. Frank records 'Softly As I Leave You', 'Then Suddenly Love' and 'Available' with Ernie Freeman. A version of 'Since Marie Has Left Paree' with Billy May is recorded but not released.

October 3
With Nelson Riddle, Frank records 'Pass Me By', 'Emily' and 'Dear Heart' for the album 'Softly As I Leave You'.

Mia with the flowing locks.

October
Frank meets Mia Farrow on the lot at 20th Century Fox. He's working on *Von Ryan's*

UK pop star John Leyton (left) with Frank and Trevor Howard in *Von Ryan's Express*.

Express, also on the TV serial *Peyton Place*. They are introduced by Sinatra's co-star John Leyton.

November 11
With Ernie Freeman, Frank records 'Anytime At All' and 'Somewhere In Your Heart'. Of the latter, Freeman comments: "That's the first thing we did that had a real heavy beat and a sing-along feel to it – it's amazing how this man, who's the greatest phraser in the world and loves to play with a lyric, felt the way we were doing it and stayed right in the sing-along groove."

November 26
Frank and The Count Basie Band link at the Sands Hotels, Las Vegas, to provide a joint concert, the first of many.

1965

February
President De Gaulle of France awards Frank the Commandeur del la Sante Publique for his humanitarian work.

February 11
The film *None But The Brave* gets a release. It marks Sinatra's directorial début (he also produces and stars) with a film about a pharmacist's mate who amputates the leg of a Japanese soldier after a skirmish during World War II. The film marks the first venture actually filmed by a joint American-Japanese company in the USA.

April 13, 14 & 22
In Hollywood, Frank works with Gordon Jenkins on the 'September Of My Years' album, recording 'Don't Wait Too Long', 'September Song', 'Last Night When We Were Young', 'Hello Young Lovers', 'I See It Now', 'When The Wind Was Green', 'Once Upon A Time', 'How Old Am I?', 'It Was A Very Good Year', 'The Man In The Looking Glass', 'This Is All I Ask' and 'It Gets Lonely Early', also slotting in a couple of sides ('Tell Her You Love Her Each Day' and 'When Somebody Loves You') with Ernie Freeman.

April 14
One paper reports Frank as claiming: "If I had as many love affairs as I'm credited with, I would be talking to you from inside a jar at Harvard Medical Centre."

April 23
Life magazine runs a special feature 'Frank Sinatra - A Visit To His Private World'. The issue proves a sell-out.

May 6
An L.A. recording session with Ernie Freeman produces 'Forget Domani'.

May 27
Frank and Gordon Jenkins record the title track to the 'September Of My Years' album.

June
Frank spends a few days in Israel filming his brief cameo in *Cast A Giant Shadow*.

June 20
Sinatra and Basie in concert at the Kiel Opera House, St Louis, Missouri. It's the first date of a six-city tour.

June 23
Von Ryan's Express is released. "This World War II suspense thriller tells of the mass escape of 600 American and British prisoners-of-war across Nazi-controlled Italy in 1943. As the commanding officer and leader of the escape, Sinatra socks over his character strongly."

July 4
On Independence Day, Sinatra swings the Newport Jazz Festival in the company of The Count Basie Orchestra, receiving a rapturous ovation from the audience though he's vocally not at his best.

July 8, 9 & 10
More Sinatra-Basie, this time at Forest Hills Tennis Club.

July 20
In Hollywood, Frank becomes the 150th celebrity to sign his name and place his footprint on the Walkway Of The Stars outside Grauman's Chinese Theater.

August 5
Frank charters a 168ft white yacht named *Southern Breeze* and cruises off the coast of New England. There's a crew of 23 plus a number of guests including Mia Farrow.

August 11
A crew member of the *Southern Breeze* is drowned when a dinghy, in which he is returning from shore, collapses.

August 18
Still on board the yacht with Mia, Frank receives a telegram from Dean Martin that reads: "I've got Scotch older than she is."

August 23
A recording session with Torrie Zito, the songs: 'Everybody Has The Right To Be Wrong (At Least Once)', 'I Only Miss Her When I Think Of Her'. Additionally, there's a Nelson Riddle arrangement 'Golden Moment'.

September 7
A benefit for Governor Brown at the Hilton Hotel, San Francisco. Nelson Riddle heads the orchestra.

September 16
Frank guests on the début of NBC-TV's *Dean Martin Show*. This same day *Marriage On The Rocks* is released. A dull, situation comedy, it features Sinatra as a middle-aged business exec who loses his wife to friend and perennial bachelor Dean Martin before deciding that he's made the wrong move. No one hates the film more than Mexicans who feel that it depicts their country as a place merely for quickie divorces and peopled by dubious officials.

October 11
Sonny Burke conducts the orchestra as Frank records 'Come Fly With Me' and 'I'll Never Smile Again'.

October 21
Frank dubs the vocals to 'Moment To Moment' and 'Love And Marriage' using previously recorded orchestral tracks by Nelson Riddle.

November 16
CBS-TV screen *Sinatra – An American Original*, a documentary about Sinatra that includes scenes of Frank, Dean Martin and Sammy Davis Jr. fooling around at a record session and at a benefit for prison inmates.

November 24
NBC-TV present the hour-long colour special *A Man And His Music*, a tribute to Frank Sinatra.

November 29
Frank records 'Moonlight Sinatra', an album of 'moon' songs, with Nelson Riddle. Tracks: 'Moon Song', 'Moon Love', 'The Moon Got In My Eyes', 'Moonlight Serenade', 'Reaching For The Moon', 'I Wished On The Moon', 'Moonlight Becomes You', 'Moonlight Mood', 'Oh You Crazy Moon' and 'The Moon Was Yellow'.

December 12
Ex-wife Nancy hosts a 50th birthday party for Frank, given at Hollywood's Beverly Wiltshire Hotel. Milton Berle acts as MC, Tony Bennett sings for his supper and Sammy Davis Jr. jumps out of the cake.

December 17
Independent Television News agree to pay libel damages to Frank for suggesting that the kidnap of Frank Jr. was a publicity stunt.

The Chairman of The Board meets The Count.

In London 1962 at The
Great Songs From
Great Britain sessions.

1966

January 17-22

Pye Records launch a Frank Sinatra Week in Britain, to mark Frank's 50th birthday and 25 years in show-biz.

January 26

Recording begins at the Sands Hotel where Sinatra is appearing with Count Basie and his Orchestra, using arrangements shaped by Quincy Jones. Ten shows are recorded between this date and February 1, the best of the performances ending up on an album succinctly titled 'Sinatra At The Sands'. Songs: 'I've Got A Crush On You', 'I've Got You Under My Skin', 'The September Of My Years', 'Street Of Dreams', 'You Make Me Feel So Young', 'The Shadow Of Your Smile', 'Luck Be A Lady', 'It Was A Very Good Year', 'Don't Worry 'Bout Me', 'My Kind Of Town', 'One For My Baby', 'Fly Me To The Moon', 'Get Me To The Church On Time', 'Angel Eyes', 'Where Or When' and 'Come Fly With Me'. Remembers Basie: "Frank found out we had a couple of days open just before we were scheduled to go into the Sands with him and he arranged to have the band fly out to Vegas from Chicago at his personal expense two days in advance, just for us to be on hand for extra rehearsals."

February 15

The Oscar gets a timely release. A movie based on Richard Sale's Hollywood novel about an unscrupulous Oscar nominee, Frank appears in a minute but meaningful role.

March 15

At the eighth Grammy Awards, 'September Of My Years' is hailed as Album Of The Year, Sinatra also winning the Best Vocal Male Performance category for his 'It Was A Very Good Year' single, which also gains a Best Accompanying Arrangement Grammy for Gordon Jenkins.

March 30

Cast A Giant Shadow is released. And it's cameo time again as Frank plays a happy-go-lucky aviator in this fictionalised biopic based around the life of Colonel Mickey Marcus who assisted in the establishment of Israel.

April 4

Frank's NBC-TV special, *Frank Sinatra: A Man And His Music*, is screened in the UK by BBC-TV.

April 11

At a Dean Martin recording session, Frank records 'Strangers In The Night' with Ernie Freeman. Legend has it that the date was hastily slotted in because A&R man Jimmy Bowen had heard that Bobby Darin and Jack Jones were both cutting versions of the song, originally a Bert Kaempfert instrumental that featured in the film *A Man Could Get Killed*.

May 7

'Strangers In The Night' enters the US charts and begins making its way to No 1.

May 11 & 16

Frank and Nelson Riddle piece together such tracks as 'My Baby Just Cares For Me', 'Yes Sir That's My Baby', 'You're Driving Me Crazy', 'The Most Beautiful Girl In The World', 'Summer Wind', 'All Or Nothing At All', 'Call Me', 'On A Clear Day You Can See Forever' and 'Downtown' all of which will form part of the 'Strangers In The Night' album.

June 6

The single 'Strangers In The Night' hits No 1 in the UK charts and clings to pole position for three weeks.

June 8

Frank attends Dean Martin's 49th birthday celebration at the Polo Room of the Beverly Hills Hotel but gets involved in a fight with Frederick R. Weisman, president of Hunt's Foods, the latter suffering a skull fracture."It was a typical bar-room brawl," explains local Chief of Police Clinton Anderson. "Though we don't have any bar-rooms as such in Beverly Hills."

June 10

At his Palm Springs home, Sinatra records a send-up version of 'Gunga Din' and has copies pressed-up for distribution to friends.

June 15

The film *Assault On A Queen* is released. Frank stars in a story about a gang who use an aged U-Boat to attempt a heist on the *Queen Mary*.

July 14

Frank flies into Britain in connection with the film *The Naked Runner* and confirms that he will marry Mia Farrow shortly.

July 18

On arrival back in New York, Frank has dinner with former girlfriend Peggy Connolly.

July 19

Las Vegas. In a four-minute civil ceremony at the home of Sands Hotel President Jack Entratter, Frank and Mia Farrow are pronounced husband

Mia Farrow.

and wife. Ava Gardner comments: "I always knew he would end up in bed with a little boy."

July 25

In Hollywood, Frank records 'That's Life' and 'She Believes In Me' with Ernie Freeman but these versions are ditched.

August

In Britain, Frank begins work on the movie *The Naked Runner*.

August 2

Questions are asked in the House of Commons after Frank and Mia are allowed to land at the Ministry Of Defence airfield, RAF Northolt, in their private plane, en route to a seventh floor flat in Grosvenor Square, Mayfair.

August 18

There's more trouble for Frank and Mia after being given special clearance by Home Office immigration officers, when leaving Heathrow for Paris on a chartered plane. The British Airports Authority declare there will be no more favours in the future.

August 28

The New York Licence Department announces an end to the 'finger-printing' requirement for cabaret artists. Frank has boycotted New York night-clubs since 1957 because the law insisted that all potential cabaret acts should be finger-printed.

October 18

Once more Frank records 'That's Life' with Ernie Freeman, this time successfully.

November
Frank plays a Las Vegas engagement and introduces Mia Farrow to the audience as "a broad I can finally cheat on", reducing his new wife to tears.

November 12
'That's Life' enters the US charts on its way to the Top Ten.

November 17 & 18
A Hollywood recording session with Ernie Freeman for the 'That's Life' album. The songs: 'Give Her Love', 'What Now My Love', 'Somewhere My Love', 'I Will Wait For You', 'You're Gonna Hear From Me', 'Sand And Sea', 'The Impossible Dream' and the unlikely 'Winchester Cathedral'.

November 22
Frank is the mystery guest on TV's *What's My Line?*

December 7
Daughter Nancy appears with Frank on the *A Man And His Music Part 2* TV show.

December 24
The single 'That's Life' reaches No 4 in the US charts.

1967

January 12
Frank throws a party at Miami Beach's Jilly's South for Joe E. Lewis, the comedian he portrayed in *The Joker Is Wild*.

January 26
Sinatra testifies before a Grand Jury regarding his friendship with Sam Giancana and his ownership interest in such hotels as The Sands and Cal Neva.

January 30-February 1
Frank records with arranger/leader Claus Ogerman in Hollywood, cutting 'Dindi', 'Change Partners', 'Quiet Nights Of Quiet Stars', 'If You Never Come To Me', 'Meditation', 'Once I Loved', 'Baubles, Bangles And Beads', 'I Concentrate On You', 'The Girl From Ipanema' and 'How Insensitive', the last four in the company of Antonio Carlos Jobim. Also on the February date Frank records 'Drinking Again' and the duet 'Somethin' Stupid', with daughter Nancy.

Fred Astaire.

February 12
At the University of Southern California, Frank takes part in Tribute To Cole Porter show, along with Ethel Merman, Fred Astaire and James Stewart.

March 2
It's another very good year at the Grammy Awards, 'Strangers In The Night' winning Record Of The Year, Best Engineered Record, Best Accompanying Arrangement (Ernie Freeman) and Best Male Vocal Performance while 'Frank Sinatra- A Man And His Music' triumphs in the Album Of The Year category.

April 15
Frank and Nancy Sinatra's duet 'Somethin' Stupid' tops both the UK and US singles charts on the same day.

May 3
Sinatra is named National Chairman of The American-Italian Anti-Defamation League because of his efforts to promote racial tolerance.

May 4
Frank, barred from Mexico since April 1966, is to be allowed to enter the country.

June
Movie star Spencer Tracy dies and Frank acts as pall-bearer at the Hollywood funeral.

June 29
In New York, Frank records 'You Are There', 'The World We Knew' and 'This Town'.

Buddy Rich.

July 2
Pittsburgh Civic Arena, a concert with The Buddy Rich Band, that's an opener for a two-week tour.

July 7
Cleveland Public Hall – with Buddy Rich.

July 9
Madison Cobo Hall – with Buddy Rich.

July 13
Philadelphia Convention Hall – with Buddy Rich.

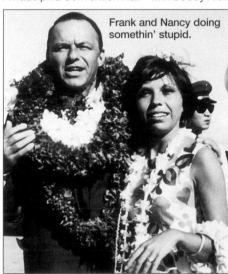
Frank and Nancy doing somethin' stupid.

July 19
The Naked Runner heads into the cinema. A spy drama, made in England, it just about makes the grade due to Sinatra's personal magnetism.

July 24
At a Hollywood date, Frank records 'Born Free', 'This Is My Love', 'This Is My Song', 'Don't Sleep In The Subway', 'Some Enchanted Evening' and 'This Town'.

August
As the tour with Buddy Rich is concluded, it's announced that the shindig has proven to be the most successful concert tour in modern music history, breaking all American indoor records by playing to 120,000 people and grossing $1,172,565.

Frank in the movie
Assault On A Queen.

The Detective.1968.

September

The Dean Martin Christmas Show with a guesting Sinatra is taped. Frank moves into The Sands, Las Vegas, to begin a three-week stint.

September 12

A top New York dentist flies into Hollywood to replace the caps on two front teeth Frank is said to have lost in a fight with The Sands' 18-stone Casino director Carl Cohen.

September 20

Frank records 'Younger Than Springtime' using an arrangement by Billy Strange.

September 21

"Frank Sinatra will be run out of town if he doesn't stop behaving as though he owns it," warns Las Vegas district attorney George Franklin.

October

Out of friendship for Vice-President Hubert Humphrey, Frank plays a special Sunday night Evening Of The Stars benefit in St Paul, Minnesota, also lining up Nancy, Dean Martin, Milton Berle, Pat Henry and the Fifth Dimension as part of the package.

October 19

New York Madison Square Garden – with Sammy Davis Jr. guesting.

November 10

Frank plays Tony Rome in the movie of that title.

"Sinatra is excellent as a flip gumshoe in this fast-moving private eye suspenser." Nancy Sinatra sings the title number.

November 13

A gala TV special featuring Frank with Ella Fitzgerald is screened by NBC. During filming, Frank gives his dressing room to his guest star. Earlier in the year, Frank was to have recorded an album with Ella but due to various problems, the idea never reached fruition.

November 22

Frank and Mia agree to a trial separation.

December 8

It's announced that actress Jacqueline Bisset will replace Mia Farrow in Sinatra's movie *The Detective*.

December 11 & 12

Frank gets together with Duke Ellington to record such titles as 'All I Need Is The Girl', 'Yellow Days', 'Indian Summer', 'Come Back To Me', 'Sunny', 'Follow Me', 'I Like The Sunrise' and 'Poor Butterfly'. The venue's Hollywood and the arrangements are provided by Billy May. Also on December 11 the *Movin' With Nancy* TV show is screened and includes a segment that features Frank in a studio setting.

December 21

The Dean Martin Christmas Show is screened.

1968

February 2

Frank opens at The Fontainebleau, Miami, for a season that will run through to mid-May, with a break in March as Frank battles against pneumonia. Also during this period he films scenes for *Lady In Cement*.

April

Frank sings at the New York Copacabana for the first time in 12 years, during the midnight show of Louis Prima's opening.

April

Frank turns in his finest acting performance for some years in *The Detective*, playing Joe Leland, a tough New York cop investigating the messy murder of a homosexual.

May 2

The Paul Newman-Joanne Woodward movie *A New Kind Of Love* opens in New York. The soundtrack includes Sinatra's version of 'You Brought A New Kind Of Love To Me'.

May 22

Oakland Coliseum Arena. A show for Hubert Humphrey and the Democratic Party of California.

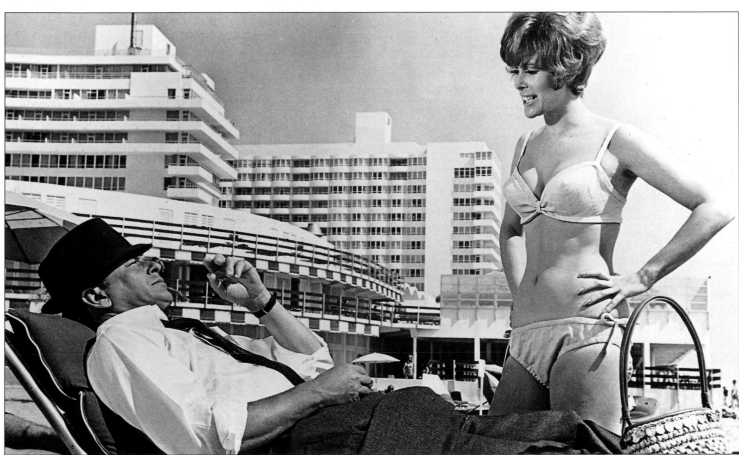

As Tony Rome with Jill St.John.

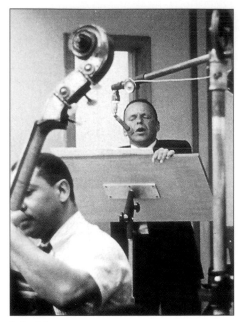

July 24

In New York, Frank records 'My Way Of Life', 'Cycles' and 'Whatever Happened To Christmas', using Don Costa arrangements.

August 3

Philadelphia, The Spectrum.

August 12

The Sinatra family - Frank, Nancy, Tina and Frank Jr. get together in a Hollywood studio to record 'The Twelve Days Of Christmas', 'The Bells Of Christmas', 'I Wouldn't Trade Christmas' and 'The Christmas Waltz'.

August 16

Mia Farrow heads for Juarez, Mexico, and divorces Frank on grounds of "incompatibility due to intolerable arguments."

September 28

It's announced that Frank will record an album of material penned by Tony Hatch and Jackie Trent. But after the duo supply the material, Sinatra eventually loses interest in the project.

November 11

Hollywood. Sinatra records 'Blue Lace' and 'Star' with Nelson Riddle.

November 12, 13 & 14

Using Don Costa arrangements, Frank records 'Little Green Apples', 'Gentle On My Mind', 'By The Time I Get To Phoenix', 'Moody River', 'Pretty Colours', 'Rain In My Heart', 'Wandering' and 'From Both Sides Now' for the 'Cycles' album. George Harrison who drops in with wife Patti, is amazed at the speed of Sinatra's ability to cut an album and asks "How do you do it? It takes us months just to do one album." Tiny Tim also attends and gets his picture on the back of the album sleeve.

November 15

It's announced that Frank is moving to Palm Springs because the smog in L.A and Hollywood is ruining his health.

November 20

The movie *Lady In Cement* is released. A sequel to *Tony Rome*, it has a scuba-diving Sinatra discovering a nude woman anchored in cement on the ocean floor.

November 25

The TV show *Francis Albert Sinatra* is screened. The guest stars include Diahann Carroll and The Fifth Dimension.

November 26

Frank opens at the Las Vegas Caesar's Palace, playing cabaret at The Circus Maximus as part of a fortnight's engagement with Harry James and His Orchestra.

December 6-9

It's no-show at Circus Maximus as Frank contracts 'flu.

December 30

Frank records 'My Way' in Hollywood, with Don Costa conducting. It's a French song 'Comme d'habitude' penned in 1967, with an English lyric added by Paul Anka.

1969

January 19

Frank flies his parents to Houston's Methodist Hospital, where Marty Sinatra, Frank's father, is examined for an enlarged aorta.

January 24

Following a few days' rest in the hospital, Marty's heart gives out and he dies, age 74.

January 29

The funeral of Frank's father takes place at Fort Lee's Madonna Church, New Jersey. Following Marty's death, Sinatra makes plans to endow the Martin Anthony Sinatra Medical Education Centre, part of the Desert Hospital, in Palm Springs.

February 11, 12 & 13

Hollywood. Time for a bossa nova recording session with Antonio Carlos Jobim using arrangements by Eumir Deodato and an orchestra conducted by Morris Stoloff. The songs: 'One Note Samba', 'Don't Go Away', 'Wave', 'Bonita', 'Someone To Light Up My Life', 'Desafinado', 'Drinking Water', 'Song Of The Sabia', 'This Happy Madness' and 'Triste'.

February 20 & 24

In Hollywood Frank records his 'My Way' album with Don Costa. Songs: 'All My Tomorrows', 'Didn't We', 'A Day In The Life Of A Fool', 'Yesterday', 'If You Go Away', 'Watch What Happens', 'For Once In My Life', 'Mrs Robinson', 'Hallelujah I Love Her So'.

February 25

With Don Costa, Frank records 'In The Shadow Of The Moon' for a Euro-only TV film.

March 19, 20 & 21

Hollywood. Frank records 'A Man Alone', an album of Rod McKuen songs, in the company of Don Costa: Songs: 'I've Been To Town', 'Empty Is', 'The Single Man', 'Lonesome Cities', 'The Beautiful Strangers', 'A Man Alone', 'Love's Been Good To Me', 'Out Beyond The Window', 'Night', 'Some Travelling Music' and 'From Promise To Promise'.

March 27

It's reported that Frank has sold his remaining 20% interest in Warner Brothers-Seven Arts and Reprise Records, receiving $22,500,000 in cash and debentures.

April 14

At the annual Oscar show at the Dorothy Chandler Pavilion, L.A., Sinatra sings 'Star', introduces Aretha Franklin who sings 'Funny Girl', and hands out the Best Song Award for 'The Windmills Of Your Mind'. Earlier, after watching a clip from *From Here To Eternity* and quipping "If I hadn't copped that Oscar, I'd still be working with Gene Kelly in sailor suits," he presents the award for Best Supporting Actor to Jack Albertson.

April 19

The single 'My Way' enters the UK charts for the first time.

May

Time for a 17-day cabaret stint at Caesar's Palace.

June 7

'My Way' reaches No 4 in the UK singles chart.

June 26

Frank attends the funeral of Judy Garland, which he has paid for, and tells reporters: "She will have a mystic survival. She was the greatest. The rest of us will be forgotten – never Judy."

July 14, 15 & 16

New York. With arranger Bob Gaudio and others, Frank records 'Watertown' a concept album. Songs: 'Out Beyond The Window', 'Night', 'Some Travelling Music', 'From Promise To Promise', 'I Would Be In Love (Anyway)', 'This Train', 'Watertown', 'Elizabeth', 'What's Now Is Now' and 'Goodbye'. The resulting album will prove one of his most unpopular releases, both critically and in terms of sales.

July 17
New York City. Records 'For A While' and 'What A Funny Girl (You Used To Be)' with arrangements by Charles Calello.

August 16
Houston, The Astrodrome. With Dionne Warwick, Flip Wilson and others.

August 18
Hollywood. A Don Costa recording date that produces 'Forget To Remember' and 'Goin' Out Of My Head'.

September
The Sinatras take over in Las Vegas, Frank playing Caesar's Palace, Frank Jr. performing at the Frontier Hotel and Nancy at the International.

October 14
A warrant for Frank's arrest is issued in Trenton, New Jersey, following a refusal to answer a subpoena to appear before the New Jersey State Commission's investigation into organised crime. Frank protests: "I am not willing to become part of any three-ring circus."

November 1
'Love's Been Good To Me' reaches No 10 in the UK singles chart.

November 5
A TV show featuring Frank with Don Costa is aired.

November 7
With Don Costa, Frank records 'Lady Day' a tribute to Billie Holiday. He had earlier attempted to record the song during the 'Watertown' sessions but failed to produce a satisfactory version at that point.

November 20
Dirty Dingus Magee is released. A comedy in which outlaw Frank comes up against bungling Sheriff George Kennedy and nobody loses except, perhaps, the cinema audience.

December 18
As lawyers argue whether Sinatra should be compelled to appear before the State Investigation Commission, one New Jersey investigator brands Frank: "A man with filthy hands who holds himself above the law."

1970

January 24
While the forecast look for the Seventies is shaven heads, Frank is reported to be in the final stages of a £4,000 transplant.

February 17
Frank appears before a state crime commission and claims that he knows no member of the Mafia, stating: "For many years, every time Italian names are involved in an enquiry I get a subpoena and I'm asked questions about scores of persons unknown to me."

April 7
At L.A.'s Dorothy Chandler Pavilion, Frank hands an Honorary Award to Cary Grant at the Academy Awards show.

April 20
Richmond, Virginia, Civic Hall – with Jerry Lewis.

May 1
Sinatra's luxury flat in Grosvenor Square is sold to film producer Harry Saltzman.

May 6
American Ambassador Walter Annenburg throws a dinner party for Frank, who's arrived in London to play two charity concerts.

May 7 & 8
Backed by Count Basie and his Orchestra, Frank plays a brace of charity concerts at London's Royal Festival Hall. They prove to be superb but are not recorded. Afterwards,

Sinatra tries to locate a bootleg copy of one of his gigs so he can retain some memory of what some feel have been his finest live performances. Sinatra fan Fred May dubs copies from his tapes and donates them to Frank's personal collection, for which he receives an inscribed gold cigarette lighter along with the singer's personal thanks.

July 9
A lifelong Democrat, Sinatra engages in a political somersault and joins the campaign to elect California's right-wing Governor, Ronald Reagan.

September 6
Sanford Waterman, the manager of the casino at Las Vegas' Caesar's Palace, threatens Sinatra with a gun following an argument about credit at a gaming table.

September 9
Frank guests on Dinah Shore's *Dinah's Place* TV show.

October 5
San Francisco Hilton Hotel. A Benefit for Ronald Reagan.

October 26, 27, 28 & 29
At Hollywood recording sessions Frank cuts 'I Will Drink The Wine', 'Bein' Green', 'My Sweet Lady', 'Sunrise In The Morning', 'Leaving On A Jet Place' and 'Close To You' using Don Costa arrangements, also 'I'm Not Afraid' and 'Something' with arrangements by Lena Horne's husband Lenny Hayton.

November 2
At his last studio jaunt before temporary retirement, Frank duets with Nancy on 'Feelin'

Kinda Sunday' and 'Life's A Trippy Thing'. He also runs through 'The Game Is Over' with pianist Bill Miller but decides not to record it.

November 6
Frank sends a one-word telegram to Las Vegas D.A. George Franklin, who's been defeated in his re-election attempt. The telegram simply says: "Goodbye". Franklin had previously demanded that Frank be barred from performing in Vegas unless he obtained a work permit.

November 12
It's reported that Frank has been forced to withdraw from a starring role in the film *Dead Right* due to persistent pain, following an operation on his hand that took place during June.

Frank meets Princess Margaret at London's Royal Festival Hall.

November 16
Frank and Bob Hope play two concerts at London's Festival Hall in order to raise money for the United World Colleges Fund. Among the

songs Sinatra performs is 'I Will Drink The Wine' penned by Paul Ryan. The shows raise $100,000.

November 18
Frank appears on TV's *Danny Thomas Show*.

December 5
'My Way' reappears in the UK singles chart and this time will peak at No 17.

December 12
Daughter Nancy weds television director Hugh Lambert in Cathedral City, California on Frank's 55th birthday.

December 31
Frank and Ruth Buzzi guest on NBC-TV's *Dean Martin Show*.

1971

January 4
In Sacramento, Sinatra attends Ronald Reagan's Inaugural Gala at the Municipal Auditorium. John Wayne, Dean Martin and Jack Benny are among the other show-biz personalities at the Gala.

February 27
'I Will Drink The Wine' reaches No 30 in the UK singles chart.

March 8
Frank is spotted ringside, camera in hand, at the Muhammed Ali-Joe Frazier fight.

March 18
Boston Hynes Civic Auditorium. Frank performs at a testimonial dinner for Frank Fontaine.

March 23
It's announced: "Frank Sinatra will retire from show business in June after fulfilling promised engagements."

April 4
Just when you felt it was safe to go back into the record shop, 'My Way' charts yet again in the UK, reaching No 29 in the singles listing. Later, the *Guinness Book Of Records* will credit the single with the longest ever stay in the UK charts, notching some 122 weeks in the ratings.

April 15
Frank is given one of the highest honours in show-biz – a special Oscar, The Jean Hersholt Humanitarian Award, presented by the Motion Pictures Academy of Arts and Sciences.

May 29
In Memphis, Frank performs as part of the Shower Of Stars Benefit Concert.

June 13
At the Dorothy Chandler Pavilion, Sinatra makes his 'final' appearance onstage, headlining at an L.A. Benefit for the Motion Picture and TV Relief Fund. Jack Benny, Bob Hope, Barbra Streisand, Don Rickles and Sammy Davis Jr also appear. Sinatra's act ends with 'Angel Eyes', the last line to which is "Excuse me while I disappear." One writer claims: "It was the single most stunning moment I have ever witnessed onstage." He repeats the performance later in the day at the city's Ahmanson Theater, where the show is recorded by Reprise but never released.

November
Frank attends a New York party for Aristotle Onassis and his wife Jackie.

November 10
In Los Angeles, Sinatra attends a dinner aimed at raising funds for Richard Nixon's re-election campaign. He sits at the same table as Nancy Reagan.

December 10
Frank achieves the ultimate in status symbols as the street outside his Palm Springs home is renamed Frank Sinatra Way.

1972

June 4
Invited to appear before a congressional committee delving into organised crime, Frank declines and flies to England.

July 18
In Washington D.C. Frank is eventually questioned by a House Crime Committee about

mob involvement at the Berkshire Downs racetrack.

July

After being subpoenaed by the congressional committee regarding alleged involvement in Mafia matters, Frank contributes an article to the *New York Times* Op-Ed page titled "We Might Call This The Politics Of Fantasy" which concludes: "There are some larger questions raised by my appearance that have something to say to all of us. The most important is the right of a private citizen in this country when faced with the huge machine of the central Government."

August 3

Frank claims High Court libel damages against two BBC programmes, TV's *24 Hours* and the radio news programme *World At One*.

October 20

Though still in retirement, Sinatra sings 'My Kind Of Town' at a Young Voters For Nixon rally in Chicago.

November 1

Frank is honoured by Israel and presented with the Medallion Of Valor Of The State Of Israel for his 'unprecedented' humanitarian efforts on behalf of his fellow man.' French philanthropist Baron Edmond de Rothschild makes the award, while Vice President Spiro Agnew attends the ceremony.

1973

January

Frank flies to Washington with the newly-divorced Barbara Marx to hold a number of pre-inaugural parties on behalf of the Nixon-Agnew political team.

March

Sinatra is the recipient of an award from the Thomas A. Dooley Foundation.

March 27

Frank presents a special award to his friend Rosalind Russell at the Oscars, once more held at the Dorothy Chandler Pavilion, L.A.

April 17

After a White House performance for President Nixon and the Italian President, Sinatra opts for a general return to work and announces that he's "retired from retirement".

April 29

Frank records 'Hurt Doesn't Go Away' and 'Noah' in Hollywood but the masters are later destroyed.

June 4/5

At Hollywood sessions with Gordon Jenkins, Frank re-records 'The Hurt Doesn't Go Away' and 'Noah' along with 'Bang Bang', 'Nobody Wins' and 'You Will Be My Music'.

June 21/22

Further recording sessions with Gordon Jenkins produce 'Winners', 'Let Me Try Again', 'Empty Tables', 'Walk Away', 'There Used To Be A Ballpark' and 'Send In The Clowns'.

August 20

With Gordon Jenkins, Frank records 'You're So Right (For What's Wrong In My Life)' and 'Dream Away'.

October 10

The day after his friend, vice-president Spiro Agnew resigns due to tax evasion charges, Frank sends him $30,000. The money is to help pay a fine and also provide expenses until Agnew accepts another job. Additionally, he loans Agnew over $200,000 to pay various back taxes, penalties, legal costs etc.

November 18

NBC-TV screens *Old Blues Eyes Is Back*.

December 10

The final Hollywood recording session of the year, with Don Costa, produces 'Bad Bad Leroy Brown' and 'I'm Gonna Make It All The Way'.

1974

January 25

The opening night of Frank's return to Caesar's Palace, Las Vegas, proves to be among the greatest in show-biz history, with scores of stars in attendance, plus the whole Sinatra family with the exception of Frank Jr.

January 26

Tina Sinatra weds record company executive Wes Farrell at Caesar's Palace, Las Vegas. Frank and sister Nancy are among those in attendance.

January 28 & 29

Two Caesar's Palace shows are cancelled because Frank has a sore throat.

January 31

Frank plays the final night of the Las Vegas date.

March 1

A one-week season at Caesar's Palace has to be scrapped due to recurring throat trouble.

March 9

San Jose Civic Auditorium. With Gordon Jenkins.

March 24

Miami, The Fontainebleau. With Gordon Jenkins.

April 8

Frank plays a Carnegie Hall date before setting off on his first concert tour for some years.

April 9-11

Long Island Veterans' Memorial Coliseum.

April 12

The film *That's Entertainment* gets its first screening in Hollywood. A retrospective of the MGM musical, it contains clips from several Sinatra movies.

April 15-16

Providence, Rhode Island Civic Center.

April 18

Detroit Olympic Stadium.

April 21-22

Philadelphia, The Spectrum.

April 24

Washington DC, Capitol Center.

April 26-27

Chicago, The Stadium.

May 5

Insurance agent Harry Weinstock claims that Frank has ordered bodyguards to beat him after an incident in the restaurant of the Trinidad Hotel.

May 7

A Hollywood recording date with Gordon Jenkins. The songs – 'Empty Tables', 'If' and 'The Summer Knows'.

May 8, 9 & 21

Using Don Costa arrangements, Frank records 'Sweet Caroline', 'You Turned My World Around', 'What Are You Doing The Rest Of My Life?', 'Tie A Yellow Ribbon Round The Ol' Oak Tree', 'Satisfy Me One More Time' and 'If You Could Read My Mind'.

May 22

It's grandfather Frank as daughter Nancy has her first child, a 9lb girl named Angela Jennifer Lambert. Frank toasts his grandchild from the stage of Caesar's Palace.

May 24

Using a previously recorded Don Costa orchestral track, Frank records 'You Are The Sunshine Of My Life' in Hollywood.

Basie – The Kid from Red Bank.

June 6

A feature predictably titled 'He Did It His Way' appears in *Rolling Stone*. It's a resumé on the recent Sinatra tour and claims that $15 seats in New York were sold for $100 apiece, breaking New York state law. The publication of the piece coincides with Frank opening at Caesar's Palace along with Pat Henry, Ella Fitzgerald and The Count Basie Orchestra. The show is booked to play nearly two weeks, the closer on every gig being a duet between Frank and Ella on 'The Lady Is A Tramp'.

Early July

Frank plays three concerts in Japan.

July 5

A concert for US servicemen is given on board the *USS Midway* moored in a Japanese naval base.

July 9

Australia. Frank plays a show at Melbourne's Festival Hall but falls foul of the press.

July 10

Though a ban is placed on his shows in Oz, Sinatra says he will not apologise for statements he made about the local press, calling them "bums" and "parasites". And Bob Hawke, president of the Australian Council Of Trade Unions, claims that Frank will not be able to leave Australia unless an apology is forthcoming.

July 11

Frank and the Australian Unions patch up their differences and the ban on his concerts is lifted.

July 13

At a Sydney concert Sinatra declares that President Nixon is pleased with the furore Frank's been causing: "because it keeps Watergate off the front pages."

July 16

The final Sydney concert is televised free of fee as a kind of goodwill gesture.

July 18

Frank flies to Biarritz after a brief stopover in London. Later he's spied in the pool at the Hotel De Palais.

September

A federal jury clears Frank of ordering his bodyguards to beat up insurance man Frank Weinstock, but awards Weinstock $101,000 damages against one of Frank's friends, Jilly Rizzo, who is given a new trial, one which ends in an out-of-court settlement.

Woodsheddin' with Woody.

September 4-11

Lake Tahoe Harrah's. It's Frank with Frank Jr. and Nancy plus The Woody Herman Orchestra.

September 12-19

Las Vegas Caesar's Palace: The Sinatra Family and Woody Herman continue to stun audiences, the final show being a Benefit for The Cedars Mount Sinai Hospital.

September 24

Frank records three songs ('The Saddest Thing Of All', 'Everything Happens To Me' and 'Just As Though You Were Here') using Gordon Jenkins arrangements. But nothing is released.

October 2

A Boston concert kicks off a full tour with Woody Herman.

October 4

Buffalo Memorial Auditorium.

October 7

Philadelphia, The Spectrum.

October 12

The first of three concerts at Madison Square Garden.

October 13

Sinatra performs a live TV concert called *The Main Event* on stage at Madison Square. But the ratings are far from good. Afterwards, an album also called 'The Main Event' is pieced together. It purports to document the New York show but actually features material recorded at various dates. The tracks: 'The Lady Is A Tramp', 'I Get A Kick Out Of You', 'Let Me Try Again', 'Autumn In New York', 'I've Got You Under My Skin', 'Big Bad Leroy Brown', 'Angel Eyes', 'You Are The Sunshine Of My Life', 'The House I Live In', 'My Kind Of Town' and 'My Way'. The back-up orchestra is Woody Herman's Young Thundering Herd.

October 29

The last show of Frank's autumn tour with Woody Herman takes place in Dallas.

November 1

New York, Madison Square Garden.

November 7

It's announced that Sinatra is to sell his estate in Palm Springs and will move to Idyllwild, west of Palm Springs, in the San Jacinto mountains. The property for sale boasts five guest houses, a tennis court, two swimming pools, a whirlpool bath, sauna and a heliport in addition to the main house.

December 31

Miami, The Diplomat.

1975

January 10-12

A three-day engagement at Harrah's, Lake Tahoe.

January 16-22

Las Vegas Caesar's Palace, with comedian Pat Henry as support.

February 14-17

Harrah's, Lake Tahoe again. This time for four days.

Sinatra with Jilly Rizzo.

February 20
Hollywood. Frank records 'The Only Couple On The Floor' but the version is not released.

March 3
Hollywood. Using Don Costa arrangements Frank cuts 'Anytime (I'll Be There)'and 'The Only Couple On The Floor', plus 'I Believe I'm Gonna Love You', arranged by Al Capps, and 'Grass', which is not released.

March 12
Frank records 'Oh Babe What Would You Say', 'You Are The Sunshine Of My Life' and 'That Old Black Magic' with Don Costa, none of which are released.

March 20-April 2
Las Vegas, Caesar's Palace.

March 23
Frank fills a 10-minute mid-day spot at The Tropicana, Las Vegas, and sings just two songs. 'You Are The Sunshine Of My Life' and 'Big Bad Leroy Brown'.

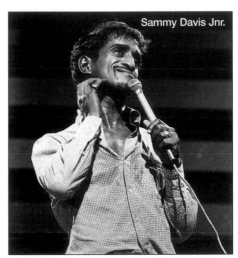
Sammy Davis Jnr.

April 8
Practically a regular at the Oscar handouts, Frank once more presents prizes and provides a speech apologising on behalf of the Academy for the various political references made on the programme, antagonising Shirley MacLaine by so doing. Eventually Frank has to be dragged onstage by Sammy Davis Jr. in order to link with the other three hosts and sing 'That's Entertainment'.

April 24
San Francisco Civic Arena. With Don Costa. The first stop on yet another concert tour that spins through to mid-May.

April 26
Portland Coliseum.

April 27
Seattle Civic Center.

May 1
Denver Coliseum.

May 3
Chicago, The Stadium.

May 4
Minneapolis, The Auditorium.

May 6
Indianapolis Market Square Arena.

May 7
St Louis, Kiel Auditorium.

May 9
Montreal, The Forum.

May 10
At a Toronto Maple Leaf Gardens concert Frank declares: "I have only two uses for newspapers – to cover the bottom of my parrot's cage and to train my dog on."

May 11
Providence R.I. Civic Center.

May 13
New Haven Veterans' Coliseum.

May 14
Sinatra flies into London with companion Barbara Marx to stay at Claridges.

May 15
The singer goes shopping in London's West End buying two pairs of boots and two dinner suits, the latter from bespoke tailors Cyril A Castle of Conduit Street, a name recommended by Roger Moore. Later Sinatra makes a trip to 10 Downing Street to visit Prime Minister Harold Wilson.

May 16
Rehearsals at the Albert Hall with a 65-piece orchestra.

May 19
Monte Carlo Sporting Club. Princess Grace hosts a jet-set party later.

May 20
Paris Palais de Congrès.

May 22
Vienna Statdhalle.

May 23
Munich Olympiahalle.

May 24
Frankfurt Festhalle.

May 25
A concert in Berlin is cancelled after allegedly playing to half empty houses at Munich and Frankfurt. Frank flies back to Britain and accuses the German press and TV of waging a scurrilous campaign against him. "They have called me a super-gangster and claimed I was a pathetic alcoholic whose career is over," he claims in a press statement.

May 29 & 30
Frank, with The Nolan Sisters and comedian Pat Henry, plays two concerts at the Albert Hall, where ticket prices range from £2 to £30, though touts ask for three times the face value. On stage he tells his audience: "Germans – I could have mentioned Dachau. They are the real gangsters."

June 1
Brussels Forest National.

June 2
Amsterdam Concertgebouw.

June 19-July 2
Las Vegas Caesar's Palace. Frank steps in as a last-minute sub for Diana Ross.

July 9
It's reported that David Bowie has been asked to play the starring role in a film about Sinatra.

Late July
There are amazing scenes as Frank attempts to book into Chicago's Ambassador East Hotel, where crowds of fans have assembled to cheer The Rolling Stones who are staying at the hotel and where Mick Jagger has booked in under the name Michael Benz.

August 1-7
Frank heads back to Lake Tahoe and Harrah's Hotel, where he and John Denver double-head a bill that pulls in over 600,000 ticket applications.

August 18
New York. Frank adds the vocal track to a Gordon Jenkins arrangement of 'The Saddest Thing Of All'.

August 19
Washington DC Merriweather Post Pavilion.

August 21
Toronto National Exhibition Center.

August 22-23
Holmden, New Jersey Garden State Art Center.

August 24
Hollywood: Using Don Costa arrangements,

Frank and Liza.

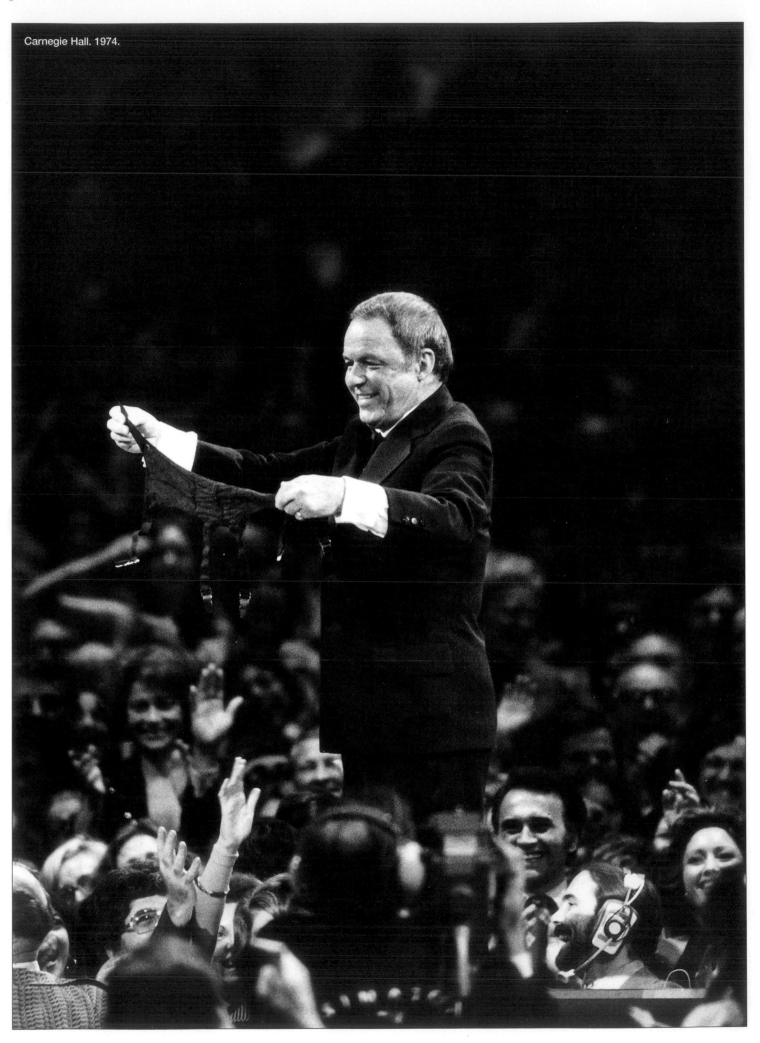

Carnegie Hall. 1974.

Frank records 'A Baby Just Like You' and 'Christmas Mem'ries'.

August 25
Saratoga Performing Arts Center.

September 4-6
New York. Frank rents NBC's Studio G for rehearsals with Count Basie and Ella Fitzgerald prior to opening at the Uris Theater.

September 5
An appearance on a Jerry Lewis' telethon aimed at raising money for Muscular Dystrophy. Frank himself donates $25,000 on behalf of his grand-daughter, Angela Lambert.

September 8
Frank begins two weeks of shows at New York's Uris Theater, sharing the bill with Ella Fitzgerald and Count Basie. The concerts gross over one million dollars. Basie recalls: "What can you say? It was fourteen days of standing ovations. That was a foregone conclusion. What else can you expect with Ella and Frank on the same programme? Slaughter!" One highlight is a duet on 'The Lady Is A Tramp'. But efforts to release an album are blocked by Ella's manager Norman Granz.

September 17
In the wake of a Uris Theatre show, Frank escorts Jackie Onassis to the 21 Club.

September 22
Philadelphia, The Spectrum. With Ella Fitzgerald and Count Basie.

October 17-24
Lake Tahoe, Harrah's. During this stay Frank meets the Russian Soyuz spacemen plus the Apollo astronauts, who attend the show and hear Sinatra sing 'Fly Me To The Moon'.

October 30-November 6
Las Vegas, Caesar's Palace. With Pat Henry and The Little Steps dance team.

November 7
After arriving at Luton Airport, then grabbing a helicopter to Battersea, Frank books into the Savoy and arranges London rehearsals with Count Basie and Sarah Vaughan.

November 9 & 10
Further rehearsals with Basie and Vaughan.

November 11
Frank, together with Sarah Vaughan and Count Basie, kicks off ten shows at the London Palladium. Again, ticket demand is unbelievable and of the total of 23,000 available tickets, half have gone to those on a priority mailing list.

November 24
Iran. Frank plays a concert in Teheran.

November 27-30
During a trip to Israel, Frank slots in a couple of concerts for the Jerusalem Foundation for Arab and Jewish Children.

December 12
Ronald Reagan, Fred Astaire, Cary Grant and Gene Kelly are among those who attend Frank's 60th birthday party, held at the home of daughter Tina.

December 31
Back in Chicago for a concert at the Stadium, Frank receives a gold medallion of citizenship from Mayor Daley, who thanks the singer for letting the world know about "my kind of town".

1976

January 15-21
Las Vegas, Caesar's Palace, the two final shows being recorded for possible album release.

February 5
Hollywood. Using Don Costa arrangements, Frank records 'I Sing The Songs', 'Empty Tables' and 'Send In The Clowns'.

Sarah Vaughan.

Medallion Man.

February 13
Philadelphia, Latin Casino. Frank's booked through to February 22 but misses several dates due to a bout of 'flu.

February 23
Sinatra meets CIA director George Bush and offers to keep him informed about his world travels and meetings with foreign dignitaries.

March
There's a spoken word recording session on which Frank contributes to two children's albums.

March 12-14
Lake Tahoe, Harrah's. Sam Butera and The Witnesses share the billing.

March 17
Again, Frank's a grandfather as daughter Nancy has a daughter – Amanda Katherine.

March 29
The CBS-TV show *John Denver And Friends* features Sinatra, plus the orchestras of Harry James, Tommy Dorsey and Count Basie.

April 4
Frank makes his first appearance at the newly-built seven million dollar, thirty-five hundred seat Westchester Premier Theater, in Tarrytown, New York. He is booked through to April 11.

Jackie Onassis.

April 10
After a show at the Premier Theater, Frank has dinner at PJ Clarke's in Manhattan, meeting Jackie Onassis, plus Peter Duchin and his wife.

April 13
That's Entertainment Part 2 is previewed. Another collection of clips from the MGM vaults, it features several in which memories of Sinatra's stay with the company are revived.

May 6
Frank issues a multi-million dollar writ against American journalist Earl Wilson, who has penned a Sinatra biography that the singer claims is "false, fictionalised, boring and uninteresting."

May 18
Frank buys Barbara Marx a $360,000 diamond engagement ring.

May 23
Las Vegas. Sinatra receives an Hon. Doctorate of Humane Letters from the University of Nevada.

May 27-30
Philadelphia, Latin Casino.

June 1
New York, Waldorf Hotel.

June 21
A Hollywood session produces 'The Best I Ever Had' and 'Stargazer' using a Billy May and a Don Costa arrangement respectively.

July 11
Barbara Marx becomes the fourth Mrs Frank Sinatra at a wedding held in Rancho Mirage,

California, the ceremony taking place at the home of one-time Ambassador Walter Annenberg. Guests include Spiro Agnew, Ronald Reagan, Gregory Peck, and Kirk Douglas. As a wedding present, Frank buys Barbara a green Jaguar XJS while she buys him a peacock blue Rolls Royce Silver Shadow.

August 21
Vancouver, Pacific Coliseum. It's Frank's first appearance in the city since 1957.

September 9-16
Lake Tahoe, Harrah's. With John Denver.

September 27
New York. To previously recorded arrangements by Don and Claus Ogerman, Frank records 'Dry Your Eyes' and 'Like A Sad Song'.

October 8
Buffalo Memorial Auditorium.

November 12
Hollywood. Frank and Nelson Riddle record 'I Love My Wife' and 'Evergreen'.

1977

January 6
A Learjet aircraft carrying 82 year-old Natalie 'Dolly' Sinatra from Palm Springs to Las Vegas crashes into a mountain. That night, with his mother's plane reported missing, Frank goes onstage for his opening brace of shows at Caesar's Palace, completing both performances and hoping that Dolly is still okay.

January 7
With Dolly's plane still missing, Frank cancels the rest of his engagement and flies back to Palm Springs, the centre of the search for the missing plane.

January 10
Dolly's death is confirmed, when remnants of the plane are discovered and bodies are seen strewn on a snow-covered mountain ridge.

January 11
Frank attends a rosary service for his mother at St Louis Catholic Church, in Cathedral City, California.

January 13
Frank, with Barbara at his side, attends his mother's funeral.

January 19
Frank records the vocal track to 'Everybody Ought To Be In Love' but this version isn't released.

January 24-30
Miami Sunrise Musical Theater, with Pat Henry.

January 28
It's announced that Frank is to star in the TV movie *Contract On Cherry Street*, based on the book by Philip Roezenburg. Frank had purchased the film rights two years earlier after learning it was his mother's favourite bedtime reading.

February 16
Frank records the vocal track for a Joe Beck arranged disco version of 'All Or Nothing At All'. But the result never appears on a commercial release. However, an update of 'Night And Day' plus a second version of 'Everybody Ought To Be In Love' makes the grade.

February 25
The night is spent at the home of Bond producer Cubby Broccoli after a flight to London.

February 26
Rehearsals begin at Broccoli's home.

February 27
Frank attends a service at Marylebone's St James' Roman Catholic Church.

February 28
At London's Royal Albert Hall, Frank plays a concert in aid of the National Society for The Prevention Of Cruelty to Children, which Princess Margaret and Ava Gardner attend. "I loathe this song," he claims as he moves into 'My Way'. "But I wish I got one like it every Friday." It's the start of a week of concerts at the venue.

March 9-14
In Hollywood Frank and Nelson Riddle record a number of tracks for a thematic album that never surfaces. The songs: 'Nancy', 'Emily', 'Linda', 'Sweet Lorraine' and 'Barbara'. He also rehearses 'Stella By Starlight' but doesn't get around to recording it.

March 17-23
Las Vegas, Caesar's Palace, with Pat Henry.

April 8
At the opening of the L.A. Dodgers baseball season, Frank sings the National Anthem.

April 21
ABC-TV screen *Frank Sinatra And Friends*, a

Frank marries Barbara Marx, July 11 1976. Top, Frank and Barbara with the Reagans and below, with the Pecks.

60-minute show that includes contributions from Natalie Cole, Dean Martin, Loretta Lynn, Tony Bennett and Leslie Uggams.

April 25
A 60-minute TV show *Music My Way*, featuring Sinatra and Paul Anka gains an airing.

Frank and Barbara at The World Series. 1977.

April 27
New York's Carnegie Hall, with Robert Merrill.

April 29-May 8
Cherry Hill, New Jersey, Latin Casino.

May 17-29
Tarrytown Premier Theater.

June 5
Sinatra receives another award from Israel. This time it's a Cultural Award, presented during a gala celebrating its 29th year as an independent state.

June 27
Frank sells a dozen French Impressionist paintings because he has decided to limit his collecting to American exhibits only. The paintings, by such as Pissarro, Monet and Vlaminck fetch £269,300.

July 4
Frank receives the Freedom Medal from the city of Philadelphia. It's the city's highest honour.

July 10
Three aircraft are hired to spell out a happy anniversary message over Long Island to Barbara Sinatra.

September
Frank returns to the Westchester Premier Theater, which is in financial trouble. His concerts help to stave off the theatre's closure.

November 12
A TV show *Tonight With Frank Sinatra*, features such guests as George Burns, Angie Dickinson and Don Rickles.

November 19
Frank stars in *Contract On Cherry Street*, transmitted from 8-11 pm on NBC-TV. The supporting cast is a strong one – Harry Guardino, Martin Balsam, Henry Silva and Verna Bloom – and Sinatra is memorable as a New York cop who wages his own kind of war on organised crime after his partner is gunned down.

November 20
Sinatra foots a $20,000 hospital bill for 63 year-old ex-world heavyweight champ Joe Louis, who is recovering from a heart operation in Texas.

1978

January 12-18
Las Vegas Caesar's Palace.

February 2-3
Frank begins another series of shows at Caesar's Palace but has to cancel after two days due to flu'. He then plays February 7 and 8.

February
A TV special *Man Of The Hour* honours Sinatra. Hosted by Dean Martin the show features tributes by Telly Savalas, Orson Welles, George Burns and Ronald Reagan who claims "He was with me all the way to the Governor's mansion. Without his help, who knows, I might have been President."

March 2-6
Yet another stint at Caesar's Palace.

March 13
CBS-TV airs *Gene Kelly – An American In Pasadena*. Frank appears and pays tribute to his old film buddy.

April 9
Around 150 stars, headed by Frank and his wife, visit Israel for the dedication of the Frank Sinatra International Student Centre at Jerusalem's Hebrew University. During his stay the singer meets Prime Minister Menachem Begin.

April 14
Frank appears on the Gene Kelly-hosted TV show *An American In Pasadena* and duets with Kelly on 'I Could Write A Book'.

May 3-10
Las Vegas, Caesar's Palace.

May 12-16
Lake Tahoe, Hurrahs.

May 21
Clan members Sinatra, Dean Martin and Sammy Davis Jr. play a SHARE benefit concert in Santa Monica, California.

May 23-29
Cherry Hill, New Jersey, Latin Casino.

June
Atlantic City. A press report states that Joe Morgenstein's club, The Sinatra Room, which has a jukebox stacked with 80 of Frank's records, and is decorated with myriad pics of the singer, is changing its name to The Trinidad Room. The switch follows a letter from Sinatra's attorney stating that the original name was not authorised and constitutes illegal appropriation.

June 17
Riverfront Coliseum, Cincinnati, Ohio. The show grosses $202,952 placing the concert at the top of the *Billboard* Boxscore chart.

June 31-July 6
Los Angeles Universal Amphitheater.

July 17
At his only recording session of the year, Frank cuts 'That's What God Looks Like To Me', 'Remember' and 'You And Me' with Don Costa. But like many other tracks recorded during the Seventies, these remain unreleased.

July 27
In Las Vegas, Frank, Barbara and Telly Savalas are spotted at a pre-marital binge for Telly's

The concert Sinatra.

daughter Christina, who is about to be wed to Hollywood producer John Kousasakie. Sinatra gives Christina a specially engraved gold pendant to mark the occasion.

August 31-September 1
Benefit performances at the Garden States Art Center, Holmdel Township, New Jersey.

September 4-6
Benefit concerts at the Hartford Civic Center pull in $371,000 gross.

September 8
At the Festival Hall, London, Frank delivers a stream of four-letter words on hearing that he will not be allowed to rehearse in the main theatre.

September 11
The opening performance of eight at the Festival Hall, with Ava Gardner in the audience. Frank is the first artist ever to play a full week at the venue.

October 13-22
New York, Radio City Music Hall.

November 2
Frank appears on the TV show *Cinderella At The Palace* with Gene Kelly. The show was originally taped in May.

November 9-15
Las Vegas Caesar's Palace.

1979

June 11-17
Los Angeles, Universal Amphitheater.

June 13
Frank receives the highest honour given to a civilian by the Italian Government, the Grande Ufficale dell Ordine al Merito della Repubblica, for promoting closer understanding between the USA and Italy.

June 15
Frank and Harry James team up once more at the Universal Amphitheatre, Los Angeles, the twosome performing their old arrangement of 'All Or Nothing At All'.

June 16
Onstage in Los Angeles, Frank gets together with Harry James.

July 16-18
Los Angeles. Frank records 'Street Of Dreams', 'More Than You Know', 'My Shining Hour', 'But Not For Me', 'They All Laughed', 'Let's Face The Music And Dance', 'The Song Is You', 'I Had The Craziest Dream' and 'It Had To Be You' with Billy May. But only the last two recordings are destined to gain a release – as part of the 'Trilogy' triple-album which will eventually include a whole album of new material plus 16 old songs that are recorded by Sinatra for the first time, along with four others that are new versions of songs he's recorded in the past.

August 3
Frank arrives in Monaco and stays at the Hotel de Paris.

August 20-22
The 'Trilogy' sessions continue as Frank records 'You And Me', 'Summer Me, Winter Me', 'McArthur Park', 'For The Good Times', 'That's What God Looks Like To Me', 'Love Me Tender', 'Just The Way You Are', 'Song Sung Blue' and 'Isn't She Lovely', the last named failing to find a release.

September 17-19
More 'Trilogy' dates, again with Billy May. The tracks: 'All Of You', 'More Than You Know', 'The Song Is You', 'But Not For Me', 'Street Of Dreams', 'They All Laughed', 'Let's Face The Music And Dance' and 'My Shining Hour', on which Sinatra comments "I can't believe we never got to this one – I've been wanting to do it for 35 years." Additionally, Frank links with arranger Don Costa and conductor Vinnie Falcone to record 'New York, New York'.

September 25
Sinatra is spotted at Heathrow but he's only clambering off a jumbo jet before catching the first plane to Cairo.

September 27
It isn't the Desert Inn, but there's plenty of sand around as Frank plays an open-concert near the Pyramids in Egypt. "It's the biggest room I've ever played," he quips merrily. The show benefits the Wafa Amal rehabilitation centre for handicapped children, a charity run by Mrs Jihar Sadat. Frank informs the elegantly dressed audience that he had sent President Sadat a congratulatory letter the previous Christmas because he was moved by the Egyptian leader's peacemaking trip to Jerusalem some months earlier. "I feel very tiny," he remarks, looking back at the Pyramids and the Sphinx.

September 29
Customers at Heathrow airport are astonished when Sinatra sits down to dine. He's on his way back to the States.

October 12
Frank receives an award from the Columbus Citizens' Committee, sponsors of the Columbus Day Parade, Frank being Grand Marshal of the 1979 Parade.

October 13-14
Concerts at the Civic Center, Providence, Rhode Island.

October 15
Civic Center, Portland, Maine.

October 22
Arena, Binghampton, New York.

October 28
Frank attends a benefit concert at New York's Metropolitan Opera House.

November 19
It's claimed that Sinatra's first marriage, to Nancy, has been annulled by the Vatican, leaving Frank free to attend Communion.

December 3
Los Angeles. Frank records George Harrison's 'Something', using a Nelson Riddle arrangement.

December 12
During his birthday party at Caesar's Palace, Las Vegas, Frank receives the Pied Piper Award from ASCAP celebrating his 40th year in show biz. Gene Kelly quips: "I remember when we danced together and I also remember when you learned to use both feet," while Dean Martin presents Frank with a diploma from Hoboken High School to compensate for the one he never earned. But, according to reports, Tina, Nancy and Frank Jr. refuse to attend the function until their father agrees not to legally adopt Barbara Marx's son Bobby, who is Sinatra's road-manager.

December 17-18
The 'Trilogy' sessions are concluded as Frank records 'The Future', 'I've Been There', 'Song Without Words', 'Before The Music Ends', 'What Time Does The Next Miracle Leave?' and 'World War None' with Gordon Jenkins and The LA Philharmonic Symphony Orchestra.

1980

January 26
Frank gets his name in the *Guinness Book Of Records* as his concert at Rio de Janeiro's Maracana Stadium attracts 175,000 people, the

largest live audience ever attracted by a single performer. At one point in the show Frank forgets the lyric to 'Strangers In The Night' but the crowd continues singing the song for him – in English!

February 2
A Frank Sinatra Chair in Music and Theater Arts is established at the University of Santa Clara.

February 14
Approximately 500 copies of the 'Trilogy' album are pre-released to link with a special Valentine's Day benefit Frank hosts in Palm Springs.

February 15
A shindig titled Frank, His Friends And His Food is held at the Canyon Hotel Convention Center, where, as Frank dons a chef's hat and apron, traditional Italian dishes are munched by a thousand paying guests, thus raising over two million dollars on behalf of Palm Springs Desert Hospital.

February 27
There's not much joy for Frank at the 22nd edition of the Grammy Awards, but at least 'Trilogy: Past, Present And Future' wins the Best Album Notes section for annotator David McClintick.

Gene Kelly with Frank and his Johnny Mercer Award.

March
Frank gains the Johnny Mercer Award from the Songwriters' Hall Of Fame for his efforts in promoting the wares of American songwriters.

March 24
Rakes Ticket Agency, in London, reports that 500 tickets, for Sinatra concerts in September, have been stolen.

April 24
Princess Grace of Monaco presents Sinatra with the Variety Club's International Humanitarian Award, at L.A.'s Century Plaza Hotel.

July 12
Frank receives an award for his efforts on behalf of the St Jude's Children's Research Hospital. Comedian Danny Thomas makes the presentation at the benefit gala.

July 17
Frank and Barbara attend the 32nd Republican National Convention at the Joe Louis Arena, Detroit.

September 8
Frank begins a series of London concerts at the Royal Festival Hall and the Royal Albert Hall.

September 22
Frank is presented with a silver tankard by the musicians who backed him at his London concerts. At Aspinall's he throws a birthday dinner party for former movie queen Claudette Colbert, who is 75.

October 5
During his act at Caesar's Palace, Sinatra verbally attacks Muhammed Ali who has just suffered a punishing defeat at the fists of Larry Holmes. As part of a 15-minute monologue, Frank tells his audience "If you didn't see that fight fiasco then you missed one of the greatest dance teams of all-time. It was like watching Arthur and Mrs Murray. I've had better fights with photographers. Phyllis Diller could have beaten Ali on the phone." Some of the audience boo and others walk out.

October 20
The movie The First Deadly Sin gets a début screening. It stars Frank as Lieutenant Edward Delaney, a New York cop faced with a series of apparently motiveless homicides. Faye Dunaway co-stars and Gordon Jenkins provides the score. Dinah Shore and Mayor Ed Koch are among those who attend the party that follows the opening.

November 30
Rancho Mirage, California. Sinatra attends a fund-raiser for the Eisenhower Medical Center. President Reagan is snapped alongside Frank.

December 9
Two tailors fly from London with a half-finished suit, which, when completed, Frank will wear at

Ronald Reagan's forthcoming inauguration concert. Cyril Castle, who has been fitting Sinatra for the past five years, says he will be returning the following day to complete the tailoring, adding that he has to get the suit back on a plane by January 3. He never discusses prices but drops a hint that none of his suits costs less than £1,000.

December 12
Barbara throws a Western-style party to celebrate her husband's 65th birthday and Sinatra's offspring present him with a huge cake shaped like a train. Music comes courtesy of a big band headed by trombonist Bill Waltrous. Guests include Burt Lancaster, Milton Berle, Dinah Shore and Johnny Carson.

December 17
The *Daily Mirror* reports that, following the murder of John Lennon, Sinatra has upped his security and before he visits the lavatories at such venues as Caesar's Palace, he first has them cleared by security men.

1981

January 2
Following Sinatra's application for a licence as a public relations and entertainment consultant at Caesar's Palace, it's alleged that the singer is once more being linked to the Mafia through a book called *The Last Mafioso*, based on the recollections of Aladena 'Jimmy The Weasel' Fratianno, a self-confessed Mafia assassin who claims that Frank acted as a front for gangland boss Sam Giacana and a Chicago crime 'family' in the ownership of a casino at Lake Tahoe, Nevada.

January 19
Sinatra pieces together an Inaugural Gala for President Reagan, an old friend, the show being televised by ABC. The show features a version of 'Nancy' with a special lyric penned in honour of Nancy Reagan.

February 5
One-time big band singer Bob Eberly, a lung-cancer victim, claims: "Frank rang my wife and said he wanted me to be transferred to a top hospital and that he would pick up the medical costs."

February 11
In Los Angeles, Frank testifies before a gaming committee in order to gain a gambling licence.

Gregory Peck, Bob Hope and Kirk Douglas speak on behalf of the singer, whose associations with alleged Mafia members threatens his application. On his show, Johnny Carson quips: "I just got word that Gregory Peck was nominated for an Oscar... for his performance at the Frank Sinatra hearing."

February 19

Frank faces a five-member Gaming Control Commission and is given back his gaming licence, lost eighteen years earlier. He is is given a reference by President Reagan who claims that Frank is "an honourable person". The Commission, voting four to one, also remove a six-month limitation of the licence, recommended earlier by its investigative arm, the Gaming Control Board.

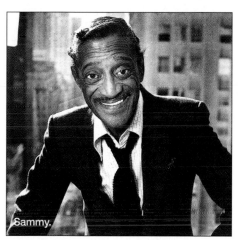

Sammy.

March 10

Sinatra and Sammy Davis Jr. play a Benefit in Atlanta, Georgia, to raise funds for the investigation into the serial killing of black children in that city. The murders continue through to late May when, with twenty-seven children dead and one missing, the police closed in on one Wayne Williams, who is eventually put on trial and sentenced to two terms of life imprisonment. The money earned at the concert helps to pay for police overtime and the cost of keeping schools open so that children can keep off the streets.

March 30

President Reagan is shot and Frank flies to Washington to offer his support and help to Nancy Reagan.

April 8

Hollywood. At a recording session conducted by Gordon Jenkins, Frank cuts 'Bang Bang', 'Everything Happens To Me', 'The Girl That Got Away' and 'It Never Entered My Mind'.

April 18

Frank attends the 25th Wedding Anniversary celebrations of Princess Grace of Monaco, the former American actress Grace Kelly, and

Prince Ranier. Along with Cary Grant, Frank makes a speech at the banquet.

July 10

Frank makes a donation to establish the Frank Sinatra Scholarship Fund which will help finance pupils attending Hoboken High School.

July 20

New York. A recording date with Gordon Jenkins produces 'Thanks For The Memory', 'I Love Her' and 'A Long Night'.

July 21

New York. During the day Frank records 'Say Hello' with Don Costa, then returns in the evening to cut 'South To A Warmer Place' with Gordon Jenkins.

July 23

Frank flies to South Africa to sing before non-segregated audiences in Sun City. He considers the gesture as a blow against apartheid, though some protest at his visit, which ignores an Equity ban, and attempt to have the singer black-listed.

August 5/8

Sinatra is booked into concerts in Buenos Aires by promoter Ramon Otega. Part of Frank's two million dollar fee will go towards homes and hospitals for children in Argentina.

August 19

New York. A recording date with Don Costa produces one track 'Good Thing Going'.

August 21

Sinatra issues a writ for ten million dollars over an interview that he claims never took place. The writ is against the *New York Star* which earlier boasted a front page billing proclaiming that it was carrying "Old Blue Eyes most candid interview ever - and only in The Star."

September 10

New York. A recording date with Gordon Jenkins. The songs: 'Monday Morning Quarterback' and 'Hey, Look No Crying'.

November 27

NBC-TV Special, *Sinatra: The Man And His Music*, with Count Basie but without studio audience.

December 10

Frank records 'To Love A Child' and a special 500 copy edition is sent to the White House for Mrs Reagan to give away at a luncheon honouring her Foster Grandparents' programme.

1982

Pavarotti.

January 25

Frank performs a concert with opera singer Luciano Pavarotti at New York's Radio City Music Hall, the twosome duetting on 'Sorrento' and 'O Sole Mio'. Both singers give their services to benefit the city's Memorial Sloan-Kettering Cancer Center and receive plaques from Laurance S. Rockefeller for their efforts.

February 8

It's reported that Frank's childhood home, in Hoboken, is still on the market after being placed for sale some six months earlier. It had been bought by factory worker Edwin Oliveri who, discovering that he's purchased Sinatra's old house, promptly placed it on the market again, hoping to get $100,000 for what is really just a modest terrace house.

April 5, 7 & 8

Frank conducts the orchestra for an album by Sylvia Syms.

April 27

At a Brighton, Sussex, auction, a tinplate model of the locomotive George The Fifth is bought on behalf of Sinatra for £3,000 who will add it to his extensive model railway collection.

July 30

Frank opens Los Angeles' University Ampitheater with a Benefit for the Jules Stein Eye Institute and other charities. The date is part of a lengthy tour in which daughter Nancy participates, opening for comedian Charlie Callas.

August 17

In New York, Frank records 'Love Makes Us Whatever' and 'Searching', using arrangements by Billy May and Don Costa respectively. They remain unissued.

Buddy Rich – drummer supreme.

August 20
Frank with the Buddy Rich Orchestra conducted by Joe Parnello plays a Concert From The Americos, an outdoor gig in Santo Domingo, Dominican Republic.

October 20
Frank and Nancy Reagan team up to sing 'To Love A Child' on the South Lawn at the White House. The function helps to promote Nancy's book about foster-parents.

1983

January 19
New York. Frank records fresh takes of 'Searching' and 'Love Makes Us Whatever' and also tackles 'It's Sunday', using a Tony Mottola arrangement. Arranger Don Costa (57) dies this same day.

January 25
New York. With Joe Parnello arranging and conducting Frank records 'Here's To The Band' and 'All The Way Home'.

January 31
At The Eisenhower Theater, Washington DC, Frank MC's the world première of *Genocide*, a multi-media documentary on the Holocaust.

February 23
'The Tommy Dorsey/Frank Sinatra Sessions Vol.1 & 2' wins The Best Historic Album category at the 25th Annual Grammy Ceremony.

February 28
L.A. Frank and Tony Mottola record a different take of 'It's Sunday'.

March 16
L.A. At a recording session, Frank tries a dozen takes of 'How Do You Keep The Music Playing' in a Joe Parnello setting. But no final master emerges.

May 1
Arranger Gordon Jenkins dies (73) at Malibu Beach.

September 21
Frank files a suit in California in an attempt to prevent Kitty Kelley from publishing her revealing biography of him, *His Way*. He also seeks two million dollars in punitive damages.

November 23
Benny Goodman is admitted to New York University Hospital for an operation. Sinatra is among the first to call.

The King of Swing – Benny Goodman.

December 11
The Variety Club throws an all-star party in Frank's honour. Milton Berle, Danny Thomas, Cary Grant and Richard Burton are among the guests, the last named making a speech in which he claims: "Frank is a giant. Among the givers of the world he stands tallest. He has more than paid rent for the space he occupies on this planet. Other than himself, there is no one who knows the magnitude of his generosity."

1984

March
Frank attends a benefit concert at Radio City Music Hall in the company of Diana Ross and Luciano Pavarotti.

April 9
In L.A. Frank presents a special Oscar to "The Godfather of Goodness" Mike Frankovitch, former head of Columbia Pictures.

April 13
In New York, Frank and Quincy Jones get together to record the 'L.A. Is My Lady Album' with a stellar orchestra that includes such musicians as George Benson, Lionel Hampton, Bob James, Ray Brown, Steve Gadd, Joe Newman and Urbie Green. The sessions take place at A&R Studios on the seventh floor of an office block and the first date produces four tracks, 'Until The Real Thing Comes Along', 'After You've Gone', 'L.A. Is My Lady' and the finally unreleased 'Body And Soul'.

April 16 & 17
The Quincy Jones sessions continue, these dates producing 'A Hundred Years From Today', 'The Best Of Everything', 'It's All Right With Me', 'Mack The Knife', 'Teach Me Tonight', 'If I Should Lose You', 'How Do You Keep The Music Playing?' and an unreleased take of 'Stormy Weather' which uses a Sal Nestico arrangement.

May 17
L.A. Employing the same Nestico arrangement but in front of an orchestra conducted by Joe Parnello, Frank records a satisfactory take of 'Stormy Weather' along with a Bob Florence-arranged 'How Do You Keep The Music Playing?' which fails to make the grade.

May 26
Frank receives an honorary doctorate degree from Loyloa Marymount University, Los Angeles.

June 29
The film *Cannonball Run II* is released. *Variety* reports: "This all-star action comedy is a shambles. Like its 1981 forerunner, it contains a lot of car chases, car wrecks and raunchy jokes which require a sub-sophomoric mentality to

1985

May 23

Frank returns to Hoboken to receive an honorary Doctor of Engineering degree from Stevens Institute of Technology. That same day President Reagan awards Frank The Presidential Medal of Freedom, the United States' highest civilian award.

June 10

Garry Trudeau's strip cartoon *Doonesbury* links Frank with the Mafia, one box depicting the singer doing it his way with the likes of Tommy 'Fatso' Marson, Don Carlo Gambino, Richard 'Nerves' Fusco, Joseph Gambino and Greg Depalma. The strip appears in hundreds of American newspapers though some refuse to carry it.

September 19

The lawsuit against author Kitty Kelley is dropped.

October 6

Nelson Riddle, the arranger with whom Frank is most usually associated, dies age 64.

October 7

Benny Goodman, Let's Dance, A Musical Tribute is taped at New York's Marriott Marquis Hotel. Frank appears on the show.

December 7-29

London's National Film Theatre screens a season of Sinatra movies.

1986

March 14

Frank appears with Red Buttons at the Meadowlands Arena, East Rutherford, New Jersey. A capacity audience pays $400,434 – a house record.

March 16

Sinatra VI, a concert at Radio City Music Hall, NYC, in aid of the Memorial Sloan Kettering Cancer Center. Also on the bill are Placido Domingo, Red Buttons, Ella Fitzgerald and The Benny Goodman Orchestra.

March 18

Harvey Fierstein, the writer of the hit show *La*

Cage Aux Folles, about a couple of Parisienne gays, claims that he is "in the talking stages with Sinatra" over the possibility of Frank taking the lead in the film version, with Jack Lemmon as co-star.

March 22

Frank's single of '(The Theme To) New York, New York' reaches No 3 in the UK chart.

Frank quits Governor's Island.

July 3

Frank reportedly throws a tantrum when his boat is delayed following his performance at President Reagan's party for the reopening of the Statue Of Liberty on Governor's Island.

August 9:

Woman magazine claims an exclusive interview with Frank, though it's a much padded affair. During the interview, the singer claims that he loves his fans adding: "It's funny, I couldn't understand how many people seemed to know my car recently, even though it has shaded windows. Then I discovered my driver has stuck a 'New York, New York' sticker on the bumper and the song title gave it away. I didn't mind, I told him to leave it there."

September 15

Kitty Kelley's controversial Sinatra biography *My Way* is published worldwide.

September 17

Frank wins £300,000 from a Swiss clinic which claims they've given him sheep cell injections to help him regain his youth. The claim is dismissed by US Judge Manuel Real as "nonsense".

September 25

Only 10,000 tickets out of 70,000 are sold for a concert at Real Madrid's soccer stadium and only the distribution of thousands of freebie

---

appreciate. It's the old boy network kind of film-making, joined this time by Frank Sinatra (playing himself) and Shirley MacLaine, in terms not endearing."

September 4

It's reported that Frank has left 15,000 fans fuming in the rain after walking out on an open-air concert in Toronto after only 25 minutes. But a spokesman maintains: "Frank took a hell of a risk singing in the rain with all that electrical equipment near him."

September 17

A party is held for Frank at the Savoy Hotel and the star raises his glass to "Bonnie Prince Henry" before guests who include Princess Anne, Gregory Peck and politician James Prior.

September 18

Following one of Frank's concerts at the Royal Albert Hall, *The Guardian* comments: "What Sinatra offers now is just something to jog the memory. When he croons quietly in his most comfortable range, he occasionally manages the kind of melodic continuity that made him famous. The rhythm swing works most frequently. But, by and large, this show by a once great artist is profoundly disappointing."

September 24

Frank and his wife send for a take-away. But the food comes from an excellent source, Chelsea's La Nassa Restaurant, who deliver the repast to the Savoy.

tickets to American schoolchildren prevents the show from being a total disaster.

September 27
A concert in Milan.

October 18
Frank records 'Leave It All To Me' but the track is never released.

Quincy Jones meets the Fan Club.

October 30
L.A. Using the orchestral track cut during the Quincy Jones sessions, Frank re-records 'Mack The Knife'. Also, he attempts Billy May-shaped versions of 'The Girls I've Never Kissed' and 'Only One To A Customer' which are never released.

November 9
Surgeons operate to remove an abscess from Sinatra's large intestine after the singer is rushed 3,000 miles by private jet from The Golden Nugget, Atlantic City, to a clinic in Palm Springs.

November 10
Sinatra is reported to be out of danger following his emergency operation.

November 16
Frank is released from the Eisenhower Medical Center in Rancho Mirage. "The doctors are very satisfied with his recovery" claims a spokesperson.

December 12
Unable to attend the 50th Anniversary Of Lew Wasserman's tenure with MCA-Universal, Sinatra sends copies of a record called 'The Gentleman Is A Champ' which is presented to everyone who is at the function.

December
At daughter Nancy's Christmas party, Mel Torme meets Sinatra, with whom he fell out many years earlier over an incident regarding one Candy Toxton to whom Mel was then engaged. But Torme comments: "Sinatra was charm itself".

1987

January 14
Sinatra heads for hospital to have an abcess removed from his large intestine. He has flown back from Hawaii, where he's been filming an episode of the TV series *Magnum PI*. The show's star Tom Selleck says that Sinatra told him that he was a *Magnum* fan and would be interested in doing the show if a good role came along. "I was thrilled and shocked," Selleck recalls. "I would never have thought of asking him."

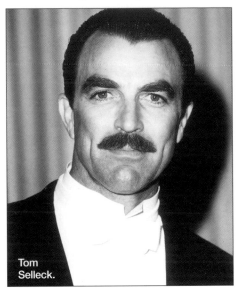
Tom Selleck.

January 22
Frank takes time-off to recuperate at his desert home.

February 9
Sinatra undergoes his third operation in five months after being rushed to the Eisenhower Medical Center, near his California home.

Doctors claim that scar tissue from previous surgery is being removed and that the surgery is merely superficial.

February 22
Cheering fans give Sinatra a standing ovation after playing an L.A. concert, his first since the stomach operation. The show, a charity concert, raises $660,000 to buy cowboy works of art for the Gene Autry Heritage Museum.

February 24
At the 29th Grammy Awards, 'The Voice, The Columbia Years 1943-1952' wins the Best Album Notes section.

February 25
The *Magnum PI* episode featuring Sinatra as a tough ex-cop is aired by CBS.

June 14
Frank begins an Italian tour with a date in Sicily and reminds his audience: "I am a Sicilian too".

June 22
Frank is in bed with a severe chill and running a high temperature after performing at a rain-soaked concert before 15,000 fans at the Roman Arena, Verona, Italy, the night before.

August 28
Newspapers report that Frank has offered one million pounds for a private confessional with the Pope.

September
An eight-performance season at Carnegie Hall in the company of Lionel Hampton.

September 28
It's reported that Frank is suing Dolly Parton's manager for six and a quarter million dollars,

Together again – but briefly

following the purchase of a house from him, which Sinatra claims is riddled with defects.

October 14
The Nassau Veterans' Memorial Coliseum, Uniondale, New York. With Tom Dreesen. A 15,000 sell-out.

October 17
The Centrum, Worcester, Massachusetts. With Tom Dreesen. A 12,100 sell-out.

November 13
Hartford Civic Center, Hartford, Connecticut. With Tom Dreesen. A 13,187 capacity audience.

December 1
At a press conference, Sinatra, Dean Martin and Sammy Davis Jr. announce that they're to mount a tour that will take in twenty-nine cities during 1988. American Express agree to sponsor the jaunt.

December 6
The Meadowlands, Brendan Byrne Arena, E. Rutherford, New Jersey, with Liza Minnelli. The show was originally scheduled for December 4 but Sinatra's music failed to arrive, causing the delay. Rock band Rush who were booked for the revised date, agree to postpone their gig.

December 12
A three-tiered birthday cake is wheeled onstage during a performance in Atlantic City, where Frank's appearing with Liza Minnelli.

1988

January 8
Frank arrives in Sydney for his first Australian dates in 14 years.

January 9
A concert takes place before a 40,000 crowd at Brisbane's Sanctuary Cove. The fee is said to be a straight million for a single one-hour performance.

January 18
Hollywood. Torrie Zito provides the arrangements as Frank records 'Leave It All To Me' and attempts two takes of 'The Girls I Never Kissed', both of which are unsuccessful.

March 13
Sinatra, Dean Martin and Sammy Davis Jr. open their national 'Together Again' tour at

California's Oakland Coliseum before a crowd of 15,470, the threesome closing the show with a twenty-minute medley. But Dino appears to be lagging at times. "Don't worry, he'll catch up," quips Sinatra.

March 15
Frank, Dean and Sammy at the Pacific National Exhibition Park, Vancouver, B.C., Canada.

March 16
Frank, Dean and Sammy at the Coliseum, Seattle Center, Seattle, Washington. A 13,927 sell-out.

March 18-20
Frank, Sammy and Dean play The Chicago Theater, Chicago, Illinois.

March 19
Frank quits Chicago's Omni Hotel when the manager is unable to provide Sinatra, Davis and Martin with suites on the same floor.

March 20
Dean Martin quits the tour due to a claimed kidney problem.

March 22
Frank plays The Met Center, Bloomington, Minnesota before a 32,000 sell-out crowd.

March 29
Frank and Sammy play Cincinnati River Coliseum, Cincinnati, Ohio.

March 31
Frank and Sammy at the Capital Center, Landover, Maryland.

April 2
Frank and Sammy at the Civic Center, Providence, Rhode Island, a 14,573 sell-out.

April 6-9
Frank and Sammy at Radio City Music Hall, New York.

April 15
Liza Minnelli joins the Sinatra-Davis tour, which now proceeds as The Ultimate Event.

May 11
Carnegie Hall, New York. Sinatra takes part in a Tribute To Irving Berlin concert which also includes contributions from Ray Charles, Billy Eckstine, Diane Schurr, Tony Bennett and others.

May 14
Frank defends Nancy and Ronald Reagan, slamming former officials who have published tell-all books about activities in the White House. "They're pimps and whores," he explains. Among those supposedly knocked are ex-chief of staff Donald Reagan and ex-Press Secretary Larry Speakes, both of whom have penned books about the Reagan dynasty.

May 27
The Carnegie Hall concert of May 11 receives a TV screening.

June 6
Hollywood. Using a Billy May arrangement that features a trumpet solo by Jack Sheldon, Frank attempts to record 'My Foolish Heart' but no final master results.

June
Sinatra sanctions the re-release of *The Manchurian Candidate*, which he had shelved shortly after the death of President Kennedy.

September 2
BBC screen *The Clive James Interview*, hailed as the scoop of the year. But the show proves to be all build-up and no substance, the actual interview being briefer than a bikini.

September 27-28
Frank, Sammy and Liza at the Spectrum, Philadelphia, P.A.

September 30-October 1
Frank, Sammy and Liza at the Meadowlands Arena, East Rutherford, New Jersey. The gross is $1,685,951.

October 3
The Ultimate Event tour plays Nassau Veterans' Memorial Coliseum, Uniondale, New York to a 15,000 crowd.

October 15-16
The Ultimate Event plays the Centrum, Worcester, Massachusetts.

October 20
In Hollywood, Frank attends a function in aid of the Princess Grace Foundation, a charity that helps emerging artists in the world of film, theatre and dance.

Backstage at The Ultimate Event tour.

October 27

It's revealed that porn king Larry Flynt (wheelchair bound since being hit by a sniper's bullet) once offered a hit-man one million dollars to kill Sinatra. L.A. police reveal that they found a cheque made out to arms dealer Mitchell Werbell and claim that Werbell was offered the contract in 1983 but turned it down.

November 30-December 4

The Ultimate Event at the Fox Theater, Detroit, grosses $1,507,275.

1989

January 17

The Ultimate Event at the Reunion Arena, Dallas, Texas, before an audience of 15,097.

January 18

The Ultimate Event reaches the Louisiana Superdrome, New Orleans, Louisiana. The audience – 11,750.

With Lucille Ball at the Will Rogers Award shindig.

January 25

Frank receives the Will Rogers Award at the Beverly Hills Hotel.

April 6

Milan, with Liza Minnelli and Sammy Davis Jr.

April 17

Frank arrives in London and books into the Savoy.

April 18

The first of five £75-a-ticket concerts at London's Albert Hall with Davis and Minnelli. *The Daily Telegraph* claims: "The older man's stamina goes all the way, He blows the rest of the bill off the stage." *The Times* reports: "To the astonishment of all, Sinatra remains an important artist and the first thing of his that looks likely to go are the knees", the *Daily Mirror* reporting: "The show could be worth the ticket price because it is

indeed unique. But £10 for the programmes was a pure rip-off." Prior to the concerts, tickets are sold at up to four times their face value.

May 3

In Dublin, Frank takes over the Horseshoe House pub for an evening, Sammy Davis Jr. and Liza Minnelli keeping him company at the bar. The threesome are in the city to play two open-air concerts.

June

Shows at Bally's, Las Vegas, are cancelled as Frank refuses to cross a musicians' picket line.

July 1

The Deer Creek Music Theater, Indianapolis. With Tom Dreesen.

July 5

The Garden State Arts Center, Holmdel, New Jersey.

September 10

It's reported that Frank and Barbara are appearing in a Revlon ad – the first time that the company have employed a husband and wife team in their advertising. Revlon claim that they were only able to pull off the deal by making a large donation to the Barbara Sinatra Children's Center, in Palm Springs.

October 2

The Ultimate Event – just Frank and Liza - plays the Skydrome, Toronto, Canada, before a 21,518 sell-out crowd.

November

Barbara Sinatra invites punters to have a fun weekend at Frank's multi-million pound home. But the fee is high, all profits going to her Children's Center.

1990

January 17-21

The Sunrise Musical Theater, Sunrise, Florida. With Tom Dreesen.

February

In Hollywood, Frank hosts a tribute to Sammy Davis Jr. to mark the multi-talented one's 60th anniversary in show business. A star-studded affair, it boasts appearances by Whitney Houston, Goldie Hawn, Tony Danza, Eddie Murphy, Michael Jackson, Clint Eastwood, Stevie Wonder, Dean Martin and many others. "I am delighted to be here at this wonderful celebration for my little friend, the best friend I ever had," claims Frank.

March 8-11

Bally's, Las Vegas.

March 24

Frank and Liza play a benefit for the Mercy Hospital, at the Charlotte Coliseum, Charlotte, North Carolina.

April 19-22

Frank and Tom Dreesen play the Fox Theater, Detroit, selling 22,890 tickets.

May 12

The Convention and Civic Center, Niagara Falls, New York.

May 14

Sammy Davis Jr., stricken by cancer and weighing less than seven stone, is visited by Sinatra who breaks into tears, telling the nurse:

"Whatever he wants or needs, just ask me and I'll be there."

May 16
Sammy Davis Jr. dies in Los Angeles. And Frank pays for the funeral.

June 14-17
The Radio City Music Hall, New York. With trumpeter Al Hirt.

June 24
It's reported that Frank has given Sammy Davis Jr.'s widow, Altovise, one million dollars to save her Beverly Hills home. Altovise and her 13 year-old son face eviction due the star's massive tax debt.

June 28
Frank arrives in Britain to play a series of concerts at London's Docklands Arena. The gigs form part of the Capital Radio/Coca Cola Music Festival and the 10,000 seats for the opening show prove an immediate sell-out.

July 3
Rehearsals take place at the Savoy Hotel, with Frank Jr. conducting the orchestra.

July 4-8
Docklands Arena, London.

July 8
In London, Frank and Barbara attend a party given by Michael Caine at Langan's Brasserie.

August 25
The Garden States Art Center, Holmdel Township, New Jersey. With Don Rickles and Pia Zadora.

August 26
Jones Beach Theater, Wantagh, New York. With Don Rickles and Pia Zadora.

Sinéad O'Connor.

August 27
Frank rebukes Sinéad O'Connor after she

threatens to walk out on a concert if the American national anthem is played. On the same stage, 24 hours later, he claims: "I wish I could have gone to see her so I could kick her ass."

September 8
The Pacific Ampitheater, Costa Mesa, California. An 8,861 sell-out.

December 3
In Los Angeles a musical tribute to Frank is held by the Society Of Singers.

December 11-12
It's the kick-off for the Diamond Jubilee tour at The Garden States Arts Center, Holmdel Township, New Jersey. With Steve Lawrence and Eydie Gorme. A 35,535 sell-out.

Ella and fella.

December 16
NBC-TV screen *Sinatra 75: The Best Is Yet To Come*, a collection of moments from the Meadowlands dates and the Society of Singers tribute, the guests including Liza Minnelli, Ella Fitzgerald, Peggy Lee, Jack Jones, Jo Stafford and Harry Connick Jr.

1991

January 23
Frank, Steve and Eydie at the Miami Arena, Miami, Florida.

January 25
The Centroplex Arena, Orlando, Florida. With Steve and Eydie.

February 8
The Sports Arena, San Diego, California. With Steve and Eydie.

February 10
The house record is shattered at the Convention and Entertainment Centre, Long Beach, California. With Steve and Eydie.

March 2
Sydney Entertainment Centre, with the Melbourne Symphony Orchestra.

April 18
Blockbuster Desert Sky Pavilion, Phoenix, Arizona. With Steve and Eydie plus comedian Corbett Monica.

April 20
The Centrum, Worcester, Massachusetts. With Steve and Eydic plus Corbett Monica.

April 21
Civic Center, Providence, Rhode Island. With Steve and Eydie plus Corbett Monica.

April 26-28
Circle Star Theater, San Carlos, California. With Corbett Monica. A $563,616 sell-out.

May 9
Olympic Saddledrome, Calgary, Alberta, Canada. With Steve and Eydie plus Tom Dreesen.

May 15
Elvin J Nutter Center, Wright State, University Of Dayton, Ohio. With Steve and Eydie.

May 18
The Horizon, Rosemont, Illinois. With Steve and Eydie, plus Tom Dreesen.

June 14
Riviera, Las Vegas with Corbett Monica.

June 22
The Sports Palace, Mexico City. With Steve and Eydie.

July 17-21
Sands, Atlantic City, New Jersey.

August 27
L.A. At Michael Lloyd's Beverly Hills studio Frank records 'Silent Night' for Children's Records. He does four takes, two with Bill Miller on piano and two featuring the keyboard playing of Frank Jr. Take three, with Frank Jr., is the one that's released.

September 28
The Spectrum, Oslo, Norway. With Steve and Eydie.

October 9-11
Three shows at Dublin's Point Depot in the company of Steve Lawrence and Eydie Gorme.

October 12
Frank stops off at Heathrow, after playing three shows in Dublin.

November 15
Nassau Veterans' Memorial Coliseum, Uniondale, New York. With Steve and Eydie plus Corbett Monica.

November 16-18
The last concerts of the Diamond Jubilee tour with Steve and Eydie, take place at New York's Madison Square Garden.

December 11-12
Meadowlands, New Jersey.

December 16
CBS-TV screen *The Best Is Yet To Come*, featuring moments from the recent Meadowlands shows.

1992

January 9
Following the screening of a batch of film clips featuring Sinatra, James Stewart presents Frank with the Desert Palm Achievement Award.

January 24
The Met Center, Bloomington, Minnesota. With Tom Dressen.

January 28
Sinatra reportedly chooses Philip Cazenov to portray him in a TV mini-series to be produced by daughter Tina. "It will not whitewash my father, " claims Tina. "It is not an eulogy but an honest portrayal of an incredible life."

February 12
It's revealed that Sinatra is the mystery saint who's been sending Catholic priest Maurice Chase a suitcase of dollar bills each week to be handed out to Skid Row down and outs.

February 14
Frank hosts a St Valentines Day party at the Stars Desert Inn Hotel in Las Vegas.

March 18
The Broward Center For The Performing Arts, Fort Lauderdale, Florida. With Charlie Callas.

April 11
It's reported that Frank's own brand of spaghetti sauce has been taken off supermarket shelves after failing to compete with Paul Newman's 'Newman's Own' brand.

April 23
Frank and Shirley MacLaine announce that they are teaming up for a tour.

May
Frank attends the funeral of his long term friend, restaurateur and one-time bodyguard 'Jilly' Rizzo, who's been killed in a fireball car crash while driving a white Jaguar given to him by Sinatra.

May 14-16
The Circle Star Theater, San Carlos, California. Four shows.

Gene Kelly at Frank's St. Valentines Day bash.

May 25
Frank's in London, staying at a £645 a night suite at the Savoy.

May 26
A concert at the Albert Hall, the first of six (26-31) in the company of John Dankworth and Cleo Laine. It's reported by one paper that the 76-year-old singer now wears a hearing aid but has to struggle to hear people talk and often mumbles replies because he can't hear what he is saying.

June 1
Frank has an after-show dinner at the Savoy with Prime Minister John Major and his wife Norma.

August 9
Frank appears at a charity ball in Monaco.

August 12
Now in the south of France, Frank relaxes at the exclusive Monte Carlo Beach Club in St Tropez.

August 27
Impersonator Nick Edenetti claims that Sinatra's lawyers have driven him to bankruptcy by forcing his show to close.

October
Sinatra is touring with Shirley MacLaine at a reported combined fee of £146,000 a night. Frank's contract contains a rider entitled Frank Sinatra's Dressing Room contents, which runs to 25 pages.

October 2
The Centrum, Worcester, Massachusetts. With Shirley MacLaine.

October 8-11, 14-15 and 30-31
Radio City Music Hall, New York. With Shirley

Gregory and Veronica Peck go slumming with the Sinatras – November 1991.

MacLaine. Of the eleven shows, eight are sell-outs.

November 7
The Richfield Centre, Richfield, California. With Shirley MacLaine.

November 8
Sinatra Parts 1 & 2, starring Philip Cazenov, is screened by CBS-TV. But Frank in the flesh is playing The Palace Of Auburn Hills, Auburn Hills, Michigan, with Shirley MacLaine.

December 12
Frank celebrates his 77th birthday with a performance at Las Vegas' Stars Desert Inn, closing with his familiar farewell spiel: "May you live to be 500 and may the last voice you hear be mine."

1993

January 9
In Palm Springs, Frank is given the Desert Palm Achievement Award, while playing at the Riviera Resort Hotel.

February
Producer Phil Ramone attends a meeting in Palm Beach, attended by Sinatra and his manager Eliot Weisman, to talk about making an album of duets.

April 15-18
Raymond F. Kravis Center For The Performing Arts, West Palm Beach, Florida. Frank and Tom Dreesen play four sell-outs.

April 20
War Memorial, Rochester, New York.

April 22-25
Sands, Atlantic City, New Jersey.

May 5-9
Desert Inn, Las Vegas, Nevada.

May 12-16
The Civic Opera House, Chicago, Illinois. The five sell-outs gross $1,125,225.

May 17
Hollywood's Capitol Studios. Orchestral tracks for the 'Duets' versions of 'Mack The Knife', 'Bewitched' and 'The House I Live In' are laid down. Sinatra's added vocals will be portions of live tracks recorded at various locations.

May 29
Scandinavium, Gothenburg, Sweden.

May 31
West Fallenhalle, Dortmund, Germany.

June 2
Derbypark, Hamburg, Germany.

June 5
Neven Schosses, Stuttgart, Germany.

June 6
Domplatz, Cologne, Germany.

June 10-12
The Westbury Music Fair, Westbury, New York. Four sell-out shows in the company of Corbett Monica.

July 1
Hollywood. Frank goes into the studio to record tracks for the 'Duets' albums, laying down 'The Lady Is A Tramp', 'Come Rain Or Come Shine', 'They Can't Take That Away From Me', 'I've Got The World On A String', 'I've Got You Under My Skin', 'One For My Baby' and 'Come Fly With Me'. Various guest stars will add their vocal contributions later.

July 6
More 'Duets' recording activities. 'What Now My Love', 'I've Got A Crush On You', 'The Summer Wind', 'New York, New York' and 'You Make Me Feel So Young' are taped. Recordings of 'South Of The Border' (with Willie Nelson) and 'My Way' (with Pavarotti) are pencilled in but fail to materialise.

July 9
Frank continues the 'Duets' sessions with 'Guess I'll Hang My Tears Out To Dry', 'Witchcraft', 'My Kind Of Town' and 'Luck Be A Lady'.

August 24
Backstage at the Sands Hotel, Frank adds a

brief coda to his duet recording of 'I've Got A Crush On You', in response to Barbra Streisand's 'I love you, Frank' remark at the end of her recording.

September
The album 'Sinatra In Paris' emerges on Reprise. Recorded at a Paris concert in June, 1962, it features Frank with a George Shearing-like combo performing neat, swinging arrangements mainly shaped by Neal Hefti.

September 12
The Arena, Convention and Entertainment Center, Long Beach, California. With Don Rickles.

October 9
Copps Coliseum, Hamilton, Canada, A charity show for the Kidney Foundation of Canada.

October 12 & 14
Time for the final 'Duets' sessions, with Frank recording 'The Best Is Yet To Come', 'For Once In My Life', 'A Foggy Day' and 'Fly Me To The Moon' on the first day, adding 'Where Or When', 'Moonlight In Vermont' and 'My Funny Valentine' on the second. Additionally, a version of 'Embraceable You' is pieced together using a live track recorded at various locations.

October
'Duets', Frank's first new album in ten years, is released. It features duets with Bono, Aretha Franklin, Barbra Streisand, Luther Vandross, Tony Bennett, Anita Baker, Carly Simon, Charles Aznavour, Kenny G and Liza Minnelli. It's recorded by means of Ednet, a system whereby studios can be linked by phone lines and none of the participating stars actually entered the same studio as Sinatra. Producer Phil Ramone claims: "It's the world's most sophisticated album."

1994

March 2
Frank is cut off in mid-sentence while giving a speech at the Grammy Awards in New York, the CBS TV programme fading away to a commercial. He had received a lifetime achievement award.

March 6
Frank collapses while singing 'My Way' onstage at the Mosque Auditorium, Richmond, Virginia.

Frank honoured on the Palm Springs Walk of Stars, 1994.

Paramedics rush in and Frank is taken to a local hospital but later walks out, following tests. "He just became overheated and passed out for a few moments," a spokeswoman explains later.

March 24
Maybee Center, Oral Roberts University, Tulsa, Oklahoma.

March 26
The Mark Of The Quad Cities, Moline, Illinois. Frank and Tom Dreesen attract a 10,000 sell-out crowd.

April 16
Veterans' War Memorial, Syracuse.

April 19-24
Radio City Music Hall, New York. With Don Rickles. The five shows include three sell-outs and gross $1,762,000.

May 10
The Park Arena, Hershey, Pennsylvania. It's a $374,485 sell-out.

May 12-15
The Sands, Atlantic City, New Jersey.

May 18-22
Foxwoods Casino, Southeastern, Connecticut.

August 4-7
The Sands, Atlantic City, New Jersey.

August 12
Garden State Art Center, Holmdel, New Jersey.

August 29
Merriweather Post Pavilion, Columbia.

August 30
'The Song Is You' box-set is released. A five CD set, it contains 120 tracks and spans every

studio item that Sinatra recorded as vocalist with The Tommy Dorsey band, along with 21 previously unreleased live performances plus the four sides that he made with Axel Stordahl during his stay at RCA.

August 31
Tanglewood, Lennox, Massachusetts.

September 1
Harbour Lights, Boston.

September 3
River Bend Music Centre, Cincinnati.

September 23 & 24
Greek Theater, Los Angeles.

September 29 & 30
The Music Hall, Dallas, Texas.

October 1
Hyatt Regency, Houston, Texas.

October 4 & 5
Jones Hall, Houston, Texas.

October 21
Kiel Centre, St Louis. A gross record.

October 28
Frank links with Jonathan Schwartz, Nancy La Mott, Tony Bennett and others on a 45 minute radio tribute to songwriter Jule Styne.

November 22
'Duets II' is released. And this time Jon Secada, Lena Horne, Antonio Carlos Jobim, Linda Ronstadt, Lorrie Morgan, Willie Nelson, Stevie Wonder, Gladys Knight, Luis Miguel, Chrissie Hynde, Frank Sinatra Jr, Patti Labelle and Jimmy Buffett have added their voices to the basic tracks laid down by Frank during 1993.

November 25
NBC-TV screen *Sinatra's Duets* programme but *Billboard* comments: "The biggest problem was that all the artists kept talking about what an honour it was to sing with Frank. But they were never in the same studio as Frank. However, the old footage, especially Sinatra with Dinah Shore, Elvis and Dean Martin, made it all worthwhile."

December 2
It's reported that Frank will quit touring following his upcoming concerts in Japan. "Frank will continue to record but shows now drain him," runs the communique.

December 19 & 20
Fukuoko Dome, Tokyo.

1995

January

Frank gets a Grammy nomination in Best Traditional Pop Vocal Performance category for the 'Duets II' album, while arranger Patrick Williams is also nominated for his work on the track 'I've Got A Crush On You'. Additionally, 'The Song Is You' box set of Sinatra with Dorsey sides is nominated in the Best Historic Album section.

February 25

Sinatra sings for one of his wife's favourite charities (for abused children) at a Palm Springs shindig, delivering 'The Best Is Yet To Come', 'My Kind Of Town', 'Where Or When', 'You Make Me Feel So Young', 'I've Got The World On A String' and 'Fly Me To The Moon'.

March 29

A record of Sinatra singing 'My Way' is played at the funeral of East End gangster Ronnie Kray.

April 1

It's announced in *Billboard* magazine that Carnegie Hall will celebrate Frank's 80th birthday during a three-day celebration spanning July 24-26. Each night's programme will be named after an album and various artists who have either worked with or been influenced by Sinatra will be involved.

May

It is revealed that Warner Brothers Records is compiling the ultimate Reprise box-set to tie-in with those 80th birthday celebrations.

"And now for my Chevalier impression"

UK DISCOGRAPHY

Basically, this discography covers every 'official' recording issued in the UK since Frank quit Tommy Dorsey and RCA - the term 'official' relating to companies to whom the singer signed - Columbia, Capitol, Reprise etc. There's an abundance of other Sinatra material available through record shops, mostly culled either from radio, TV or live performances or from out-of-copyright recordings. And though some of these releases are excellent recordings, many are variable in terms of sound quality, while others are downright unlistenable. So be warned.

Singles

A Lovely Way To Spend An Evening/I Couldn't Sleep A Wink Last Night
Columbia DB 2141 May 1944

All Or Nothing At All/Ciribiribin
Columbia DB 2145 June 1945

You'll Never Know/Sunday, Monday Or Always
Columbia DB 2149 June 1945

From The Bottom Of My Heart/Here Comes The Night
Columbia DB 2150 June 1945

Saturday Night/Embraceable You
Columbia DB 2176 July 1945

If You Are But A Dream/Kiss Me Again
Columbia DB 2181 July 1945

When Your Lover Has Gone/She's Funny That Way
Columbia DB 2186 Sept 1945

There's No You/Cradle Song
Columbia DB 2190 Oct 1945

I Begged Her/I Fall In Love Too Easily
Columbia DB 2197 Nov 1945

Ol' Man River/Stormy Weather
12" Columbia DX 1216 Nov 1945

What Makes The Sunset?/The Charm Of You
Columbia DB 2200 Jan 1946

Nancy (With The Laughing Face)/A Friend Of Yours
Columbia DB 2202 Feb 1946

These Foolish Things/You Go To My Head
Columbia DB 2209 Apl 1946

I Dream Of You/Someone To Watch Over Me
Columbia DB 2214 May 1946

Homesick, That's All/Oh What It Seemed To Be
Columbia DB 2216 June 1946

You Are Too Beautiful/Day By Day
Columbia 2224 July 1946

I Only Have Eyes For You/I Don't Know Why
Columbia DB 2226 Aug 1946

Begin The Beguine/All Through The Day
Columbia DB 2227 Aug 1946

I Fall In Love With You Ev'ry Day/Paradise
Columbia DB 2238 Nov 1946

Silent Night, Holy Night/White Christmas
Columbia DB 2237 Dec 1946

Five Minutes More/Try A Little Tenderness
Columbia DB 2275 Jan 1947

The Things We Did LastSummer/Somewhere In The Night
Columbia DB 2283 Feb 1947

September Song/Souvenirs
Columbia DB 2286 Feb 1947

Time After Time/It's The Same Old Dream
Columbia DB 2296 March 1947

Oh What A Beautiful Morning/The Girl That I Marry
Columbia DB 2313 June 1947

People Will Say We're In Love/They Say It's Wonderful
Columbia DB 2307 July 1947

There's No Business Like Show Business/Mam'selle
Columbia DB 2321 Aug 1947

All Of Me/I'm Sorry I Made You Cry
Columbia DB 2330 Sept 1947

Always/The Moon Is Yellow
Columbia DB 2339 Oct 1947

I Love You (Ich Liebe Dich)/Stella By Starlight
Columbia DB 2346 Nov 1947

One Love/Poinciana (Song Of The Tree)
Columbia DB 2357 Nov 1947

Sweet Lorraine
(with The Metronome All Stars)/reverse by Nat Cole and June Christy Columbia DB 2355 Nov 1947

Christmas Dreaming/I'll Make Up For Everything
Columbia DB 2376 Dec 1947

The Stars Will Remember (So Will I)/The Coffee Song
Columbia DB 2376 Jan 1948

It All Came True/Mean To Me
Columbia DB 2381 Feb 1948

How Deep Is The Ocean/Home On The Range
Columbia DC 385 Feb 1948

Falling In Love With Love/My Love For You
Columbia DB 2388 March 1948

S'posin'/How Deep Is The Ocean
Columbia DB 2403 May 1948

But Beautiful/My Cousin Louella
Columbia DB 2423 July 1948

We Just Couldn't Say Goodbye/If I Only Had A Match
Columbia DB 2431 Aug 1948

That Old Feeling/Nature Boy
Columbia DC 428 Aug 1948

Adeste Fideles/Jingle Bells
Columbia DC 431 Oct 1948

Everybody Loves Somebody/What'll I Do?
Columbia DB 2459 Nov 1948

It Only Happens When I Dance With You/A Fella With An Umbrella
Columbia DB2471 Jan 1949

While The Angelus Was Ringing/When Is Sometime
Columbia DB 2507 March 1949

If You Stub Your Toe On The Moon/Sunflower
Columbia DB 2522 April 1949

No Orchids For My Lady/Almost Like Being In Love
Columbia DB 2531 June 1949

Bop Goes My Heart/Just For Now
Columbia DB 2550 July 1949

A Little Learnin' Is A Dangerous Thing Pts 1 & 2 (duet with Pearl Bailey)
Columbia DB 2567 Oct 1949

That Lucky Old Sun/Let Her Go Let Her Go Let Her Go
Columbia DB 2630 Jan 1950

It Happens Every Spring/If I Ever Love Again
Columbia DB 2644 Feb 1950

Chattanooga Shoe Shine Boy/The Old Master Painter
Columbia DB 2664 April 1950

If I Loved You/You'll Never Walk Alone
Columbia DB 2705 July 1950

Soliloquy Pts 1 & 2
12" Columbia DX 1666 July 1950

Goodnight Irene/My Blue Heaven
Columbia DB 2737 Oct 1950

One Finger Melody/American Beauty Rose
Columbia DB 2779 Dec 1950

Life Is So Peculiar/Nevertheless
Columbia DB 2790 Jan 1951

If Only She'd Look My Way/London By Night
Columbia LB 104 March 1951

Mama Will Bark (with Dagmar)/Love Means Love (with Rosemary Clooney)
Columbia DB 2894 Aug 1951

Love Me/Castle Rock (with Harry James)
Columbia DB 2934 Oct 1951

When You're Smiling/Farewell, Farewell To Love
Columbia DB 2987 Jan 1952

It's A Long Way/Deep Night
Columbia DB 3016 March 1952

Luna Rossa/Tennessee Newsboy
Columbia DB 3144 Sept 1952

Walking In The Sunshine/Bim Bam Baby
Columbia DB 3175 Nov 1952

Birth Of The Blues/Why Try To Change Me Now
Columbia DB 3257 and SCM 5052 Apl 1953

You Do Something To Me/Lover
Columbia DB 3270 and SCM 5060 May 1953

Lean Baby/I'm Walking Behind You
Capitol CL 13924 Jun 1953

I Whistle A Happy Tune/Hello Young Lovers
Columbia DB 3347 Oct 1953

I Love You/Don't Worry 'Bout Me
Capitol CL 13980 Oct 1953

From Here To Eternity/My One And Only Love
Capitol CL 14023 Dec 1953

Santa Claus Is Comin' To Town/My Girl
Columbia DB 3390 and SCM 5052 Dec 1953

South Of The Border/I've Got The World On A String
Capitol CL 14031 Jan 1954

Young At Heart/Take A Chance
Capitol CL 14064 Mar 1954

Three Coins In The Fountain/I Could Have Told You
Capitol CL 14120 July 1954

Half As Lovely/Rain (Falling From The Sky)
Capitol CL 14152 Sept 1954

My Blue Heaven/Should I
Philips PB 364 Nov 1954

When I Stop Loving You/It Worries Me
Capitol CL 14188 Nov 1954

The Christmas Waltz/White Christmas
Capitol CL 14174 Dec 1954

Someone To Watch Over Me/The Gal That Got Away
Capitol CL 14221 Jan 1955

Melody Of Love/Gonna Live Till I Die
Capitol CL 14238 Feb 1955

S'posin'/How Deep Is The Ocean
Columbia DB 3575 and SCM 5167 Feb 1955

You My Love/Just One Of Those Things
Capitol CL 14240 Feb 1955

It's Only A Paper Moon/When You're Smiling
Philips PB 363 Feb 1955

Don't Change Your Mind About Me/Why Should I Cry Over You?
Capitol CL 14270 May 1955

Two Hearts, Two Kisses/From The Bottom To The Top
Capitol CL 14292 May 1955

Learnin' The Blues/If I Had Three Wishes
Capitol CL 14296 June 1955

Not As A Stranger/How Could You Do A Thing Like That To Me
Capitol CL 14326 Sep 1955

My Funny Valentine/I Get A Kick Out Of You
Capitol CL 14352 Oct 1955

It Never Entered My Mind/In The Wee Small Hours
Capitol CL 14360 Nov 1955

Same Old Saturday Night/Fairy Tale
Capitol CL 14373 Nov 1955

Love And Marriage/Look To Your Heart
Capitol CL 14503 Jan 1956

(Love Is) The Tender Trap/Weep They Will
Capitol CL 14511 Apl 1956

You'll Get Yours/Flowers Mean Forgiveness
Capitol CL 14564 Apl 1956

Five Hundred Guys/How Little We Know
Capitol CL 14584 Jun 1956

Johnny Concho Theme (Wait For Me)/Hey, Jealous Lover
Capitol CL 14607 Jul 1956

Our Town/The Impatient Years
Capitol CL 14620 Aug 1956

Mind If I Make Love To You/Who Wants To Be A Millionaire (with Celeste Holm)
Capitol CL 14644 Nov 1956

Well Did You Evah (with Bing Crosby)/
reverse by Bing Crosby
Capitol CL 14645 Nov 1956

You're Sensational/You Forgot All The Words
Capitol CL 14646 Nov 1956

Can I Steal A Little Love/Your Love For Me
Capitol CL 14696 Mar 1957

Crazy Love/So Long My Love
Capitol CL 14719 May 1957

You're Cheatin' Yourself/Something Wonderful Happens In Summer
Capitol CL 14750 July 1957

Once In Love With Amy/I Am Loved
Philips PB 734 Sep 1957

All The Way/Chicago
Capitol CL 14900 Nov 1957

Full Moon And Empty Arms/Autumn In New York
Philips PB 756 Nov 1957

Jingle Bells/Mistletoe And Holly
Capitol CL 14804 Nov 1957

White Christmas/Christmas Dreaming
Philips PB 764 Dec 1957

I Could Write A Book/Nevertheless
Fontana H 109 Jan 1958

Witchcraft/Tell Her You Love Her
Capitol 14919 Jan 1958

Nothing In Common/How Are Ya Fixed For Love (both with Keeley Smith)
Capitol CL 14863 May 1958

The Song From Kings Go Forth (Monique)/The Same Old Song And Dance
Capitol CL 14904 Aug 1958

If I Forget You/I'm A Fool To Want You
Fontana H 140 Sep 1958

Mr Success/Sleep Warm
Capitol CL 14956 Oct 1958

French Foreign Legion/Time After Time
Capitol CL 14997 Mar 1959

To Love And Be Loved/Live It Up
Capitol CL 15006 Apl 1959

High Hopes/All My Tomorrows
Capitol CL 15052 July 1959

Talk To Me/They Came To Cordura
Capitol CL 15086 Oct 1959

It's Nice To Go Trav'ling/Brazil
Capitol CL 15116 Feb 1960

River Stay 'Way From My Door/It's Over, It's Over, It's Over
Capitol CL 15135 June 1960

Nice'n'Easy/This Was My Love
Capitol CL15150 Sep 1960

Ol' Macdonald/You'll Always Be The One I Love
Capitol CL 15168 Nov 1960

My Blue Heaven/Sentimental Baby
Capitol CL 15193 Apl 1961

American Beauty Rose/Sentimental Journey
Capitol CL 15218 Sep 1961

Granada/The Curse Of An Aching Heart
Reprise R 20010 Sep 1961

The Coffee Song/A Foggy Day
Reprise R 20035 Nov 1961

Pocketful Of Miracles/Name It And It's Yours
Reprise R 20040 Feb 1962

The Moon Was Yellow/I've Heard That Song Before
Capitol CL 15240 Feb 1962

Ev'rybody's Twistin'/Nothing But The Best
Reprise R20063 Apl 1962

I'll Remember April/Five Minutes More
Capitol CL 15252 May 1962

I'll Be Seeing You/Without A Song
Reprise R 20053 June 1962

One For My Baby/Willow Weep For Me
Capitol CL 15258 July 1962

Hidden Persuasion/I Love Paris
Capitol CL 15265 Aug 1962

Goody Goody/Love Is Just Around The Corner
Reprise R 20092 Aug 1962

Me And My Shadow (with Sammy Davis Jr.)/(Reverse by Sammy Davis Jr.)
Reprise R 20128 Nov 1962

My Kind Of Girl/Please Be Kind
Reprise R 20148 Feb 1963

Call Me Irresponsible/Tina
Reprise R 20151 May 1963

Come Blow Your Horn/I Have Dreamed
Reprise R 20184 Aug 1963

(You Brought) A New Kind Of Love (To Me)/Love Isn't Just For The Young
Reprise R20209 Nov 1963

Have Yourself A Merry Little Christmas/I'll Be Home For Christmas
3Capitol CL 15329 Dec 1963

The Oldest Established (Permanent Crap Game In New York)/Fugue For Tinhorns
(with Bing Crosby and Dean Martin)
Reprise R 20217 Dec 1963

Have Yourself A Merry Little Christmas/(Christmas Medley)
Reprise R 20243 Dec 1963

Some Enchanted Evening (with Rosemary Clooney)**/So In Love** (with Keely Smith)
Reprise R20285 Mar 1964

My Kind Of Town/I Like To Lead When I Dance
Reprise R20279 Aug 1964

Softly As I Leave You/Then Suddenly Love
Reprise R20301 Oct 1964

Hello Dolly/I Wish You Love
Reprise R20351 Sep 1964

Little Drummer Boy/I Heard The Bells On Christmas Day
Reprise R20355 Nov 1964

Somewhere In Your Heart/I Can't Believe I'm Losing You
Reprise R23028 Jan 1965

Anytime At All/Available
Reprise R20400 Mar 1965

Tell Her (You Love Her Each Day)/Here's To The Losers
Reprise R20373 Jun 1965

Forget Domani/Emily
Reprise R20380 Jul 1965

When Somebody Loves You/When I'm Not Near The Girl I Love
Reprise R20398 Oct 1965

It Was A Very Good Year/Moment To Moment
Reprise R 20429 Jan 1966

There Are Such Things/I'll Never Smile Again
Reprise 23050 Jan 1966

Strangers In The Night/My Kind Of Town
Reprise R23052 May 1966
Reissued on K 14043 (Jun 1971)

Summer Wind/You Make Me Feel So Young
Reprise RS20509 Sep 1966

That's Life/I've Got You Under My Skin
Reprise RS20531 Nov 1966

Somethin' Stupid (with Nancy Sinatra)**/Call Me**
Reprise RS23168 Mar 1967
Reissued on K14044 (Jun 1971)

The World We Knew (Over And Over)/ You Are There
Reprise RS20610 Aug 1967

This Town/This Is My Love
Reprise RS20631 Nov 1967

I Can't Believe That I'm Losing You/How Old Am I
Reprise RS20677 May 1968

(You Are) My Way Of Life/Cycles
Reprise RS20764 Sep 1968

Whatever Happened To Christmas/I Wouldn't Trade Christmas (with Frank Jr., Nancy and Tina Sinatra)
Reprise RS20790 Nov 1968

Rain In My Heart/Star
Reprise RS20798 Jan 1969

My Way/Blue Lace
Reprise RS20817 Mar 1969
Reissued on K14008 (Jun 1971)

Love's Been Good To Me/A Man Alone
Reprise RS20852 Sep 1969

I Would Be In Love Anyway/Watertown
Reprise RS20895 May 1970

I Will Drink The Wine/Sunrise In The Morning
Reprise RS23487 Feb 1971
Reissued on K14069 (Feb 1971)

Lady Day/What Now My Love
Reprise K14098 Jul 1971

Rain In My Heart/The Train
Reprise K14131 Nov 1971

All The Way/Goin' Out Of My Head
Reprise K14177 Jun 1972

Let Me Try Again/Send In The Clowns
Reprise K14304 Nov 1973

Bad Bad Leroy Brown/I'm Gonna Make It All The Way
Reprise R14326 Mar 1974

You Will Be My Music/Winners
Reprise K14318 Jul 1974

You Turned My World Around/Satisfying Me
Reprise K14362 Aug 1974

Anytime (I'll Be There)/The Hurt Doesn't Go Away
Reprise K14393 May 1975

Believe Me I'm Gonna Love You/The Only Couple On The Floor
Reprise K14400 Aug 1975

I've Got You Under My Skin/The House I Live In
Reprise K14420 Apl 1976

I Sing The Songs/Empty Tables
Reprise K14427 Jul 1976

Strangers In The Night/Love's Been Good To Me/Softly As I Leave You/ Let Me Try Again
Reprise K14398 Sep 1976

Star Gazer/The Best I Ever Had
Reprise K14445 Nov 1976

Somethin' Stupid (with Nancy Sinatra)/ reverse by Nancy Sinatra
Private Stock PVT 79 Nov 1976

Christmas Memories/A Baby Just Like Yourself/Have Yourself A Merry Little Christmas/Whatever Happens At Christmas
Reprise K14458 Dec 1976

My Way/Strangers In The Night/Cycles
Reprise K14474 Mar 1977

Everybody Ought To Be In Love/Night And Day
Reprise K14475 May 1977

Come Fly With Me/Witchcraft
Capitol CL 15976 Apl 1978

Theme From New York, New York/ That's What God Looks Like To Me
Reprise K14502 Jul 1980

Say Hello/A Good Thing Going
Reprise K14513 Nov 1981

Bang Bang (My Baby Shot Me Down)/It Was A Very Good Year
Reprise K14515 Jan 1982

To Love A Child/That's What God Looks Like To Me
Reprise 929003 Dec 1982

New York, New York/My Kind Of Town/ LA Is My Lady
12" Reprise K14502T Feb 1986

Strangers In The Night/In The Wee Small Hours
7" Reprise W8699 Apl 1986

Strangers In The Night/In The Wee Small Hours/Last Night When We Were Young
12" Reprise W 8699T Apl 1986

My Way/Cycles
Reprise W 0163 Apl 1993

My Way/Cycles/Love And Marriage
CD Reprise W 0163CD Apl 1993

I've Got You Under My Skin (duet with Bono)/reverse by Bono
Island IS 578 also on CD CID 578 Nov 1993

EPs

Frank Sinatra
HMV 7EG 8070 Dec 1954

Songs For Young Lovers No.1
Capitol EAP 1-488 Dec 1954

Songs For Young Lovers No.2
Capitol EAP 2-488 Jan 1955

Songs From Young At Heart
Capitol EAP 1-571 Feb 1955

Frank Sinatra
Columbia SEG 7565 Feb 1955

Sinatra Serenade
Columbia SEG 7582 Apl 1955

Frankie's Favourites
Columbia SEG 7597 Jun 1955

Session With Sinatra
Capitol EAP 1-629 Jul 1955

Melody Of Love
Capitol EAP 1-590 Sep 1955

Moonlight Sinatra
HMV 7EG 8128 Oct 1955

Sing And Dance With Frank Sinatra
Philips BBE 12016 Feb 1956

Sing And Dance With Frank Sinatra
Philips BBE 12058 Aug 1956

Our Town
Capitol EAP 1025 Aug 1956

In The Wee Small Hours No.1
Capitol EAP 1-581 Feb 1957

In The Wee Small Hours No. 2
Capitol EAP 2-581 Feb 1957

Hey Jealous Lover
Capitol EAP 1-800 Mar 1957

In The Wee Small Hours No.3
Capitol EAP 3-581 Apl 1957

In The Wee Small Hours No.4
Capitol EAP 4-581 May 1957

Frank Sinatra Sings Songs From Carousel
Philips BBE 12152 Dec 1957

Songs For Swingin' Lovers No.1
Capitol EAP 1-653 Feb 1958

Lover
Fontana TFE 17012 Mar 1958

Songs For Swingin' Lovers No.2
Capitol EAP 2-653 Mar 1958

Songs For Swingin' Lovers No.3
Capitol EAP 3-653 Apl 1958

Songs For Swingin' Lovers No.4
Capitol EAP 4-653 May 1958

Anchors Aweigh
Fontana TFE 17043 Jun 1958

The Lady Is A Tramp
Capitol EAP 1-1013 Jul 1958

Mad About You
Fontana TFE 17023 Jul 1958

Fools Rush In
Fontana TFE 17037 Sep 1958

The Nearness Of You
Philips BBE 12182 Oct 1958

Where Are You? Part 1
Capitol EAP 1-855 Nov 1958

Where Are You? Part 2
Capitol EAP 2-855 Nov 1958

Where Are You? Part 3
Capitol EAP 3-855 Nov 1958

Where Are You? Part 4
Capitol EAP 4-855 Nov 1958

I Am Loved
Fontana TFE 17038 Dec 1958

Sinatra, Bailey and James
Fontana TFE 17028 Feb 1959

Frank Sinatra Sings For Only The Lonely
Capitol EAP 1-1053 Mar 1959

We're In Love
Fontana TFE 17042 Jul 1959

Come Fly With Me Part 1
Capitol EAP 1-920 Jul 1959

Come Fly With Me Part 2
Capitol EAP 2-920 Jul 1959

Come Fly With Me Part 3
Capitol EAP 3-920 Jul 1959

Come Fly With Me Part 4
Capitol EAP 4-920 Jul 1959

Dream
Fontana TFE 17158 Sep 1959

Frankie!
Fontana TFE 17182 Oct 1959

Come Dance With Me Part 1
Capitol EAP 1-1069 Oct 1959

Come Dance With Me Part 2
Capitol EAP 2-1069 Oct 1959

Come Dance With Me Part 3
Capitol EAP 3-1069 Oct 1959

High Hopes
Capitol EAP 1-1224 Dec 1959

The Voice No.1
Fontana TFE 17181 Jan 1960

No One Cares
Capitol EAP 1-1221 Feb 1960

Talk To Me
Capitol EAP 1-1348 Mar 1960

The Song Is You
Fontana TFE 17253 Mar 1960

No One Cares No.2
Capitol EAP 2-1221 Jun 1960

I've Got A Crush On You
Fontana TFE 17254 Jun 1960

They Say It's Wonderful
Fontana TFE 17255 Jul 1960

No One Cares No.3
Capitol EAP 3-1221 Sep 1960

Melancholy Baby
Fontana TFE 17274 Sep 1960

Among My Souvenirs
Fontana TFE 17272 Oct 1960

All The Way
Capitol EAP 20062 Dec 1960

Embraceable You
Fontana TFE 17286 Jan 1961

I Dream Of You
Fontana TFE 17284 Mar 1961

You Go To My Head
Fontana TFE 17256 Apl 1961

Bye Baby!
Fontana TFE 17273 Jul 1961

Five Minutes More
Fontana TFE 17280 Sep 1961

Jingle Bells
Philips BBE 12495 Dec 1961

Frank Sinatra Hit Parade Vol.1
Reprise R 30001 Feb 1962

London By Night
Capitol EAP 20389 Aug 1962

Sings Jimmy Van Heusen and Sammy Cahn
Capitol EAP 1-20415 Mar 1963

Sings Richard Rodgers and Lorenz Hart
Capitol EAP 1-20416 Apl 1963

Sings Cole Porter
Capitol EAP 1-20419 May 1963

Sings George Gershwin
Capitol EAP 1-20428 Jun 1963

Strings And Brass
Reprise R 30003 Jul 1963

Sings Johnny Mercer
Capitol EAP 1-20427 Jul 1963

Sings Harold Arlen
Capitol EAP 1-20426 Aug 1963

Sings Jimmy McHugh
Capitol EAP 1-20425 Sep 1963

I Remember Tommy Vol.1
Reprise R 30007 Sep 1963

Sinatra-Basie
Reprise R 30008 Oct 1963

Sings Jule Styne
Capitol 1-20424 Oct 1963

Sings Vernon Duke
Capitol 1-20423 Oct 1963

The Concert Sinatra Vol.1
Reprise R 30011 Nov 1963

Sinatra Soundtracks
Reprise R 30012 Nov 1963

Sings Irving Berlin
Capitol EAP 1-20422 Dec 1963

Sinatra-Basie Vol.2
Reprise R 30016 Feb 1964

Sinatra's Sinatra
Reprise 30019 Jul 1964

South Pacific Vol.1 (with others)
Reprise R 30021 Jul 1964

And Starring Frank Sinatra Vol.1
Capitol EAP 1-20619 Sep 1964

And Starring Frank Sinatra Vol.2
Capitol EAP 2-20619 Oct 1964

Sinatra With Strings
Reprise R 30022 Oct 1964

Kiss Me Kate (with others)
Reprise 30023 Oct 1964

South Pacific Vol.2 (one track only)
Reprise R 30024 Oct 1964

Finian's Rainbow (one track only)
Reprise R 30025 Oct 1964

Have Yourself A Merry Little Christmas
(one track only)
Reprise R 30029 Nov 1964

Sinatra And Swingin' Brass
Reprise R 30030 Nov 1964

Guys And Dolls (two tracks only)
Reprise 30032 Nov 1964

And Starring Frank Sinatra Vol.3
Capitol EAP 3-20619 Nov 1964

Sinatra Sings Academy Award Winners
Reprise R 30035 Apl 1965

Robin And The Seven Hoods (with others)
Reprise R 30039 Apl 1965

It Might As Well Be Swing Vol.1
Reprise R 30041 Apl 1965

Frank Sinatra's Story Of Love Vol.1
Capitol EAP 1-20653 May 1965

Frank Sinatra's Story Of Love Vol.2
Capitol EAP 2-20653 Jun 1965

It Might As Well Be Swing Vol.2
Reprise R 30047 Sep 1965

Dear Heart
Reprise R 30049 Oct 1965

Frank Sinatra's Story of Love Vol.3
Capitol EAP 3-20653 Oct 1965

Frank Sinatra's Story Of Love Vol.4
Capitol EAP 4-20653 Nov 1965

More Sinatra-Basie
Reprise R 30054 Nov 1965

Frank Sinatra's Story Of Love Vol.5
Capitol EAP 5-20653 Dec 1965

Hello Dolly!
Reprise R 30057 Dec 1965

Once Upon A Time
Reprise R 30058 Feb 1966

Frank Sinatra's Story Of Love Vol.6
Capitol EAP 6-20653 Feb 1966

Frank Sinatra's Story Of Love Vol.7
Capitol EAP 7-20653 Mar 1966

It Was A Very Good Year
Reprise R 30065 May 1966

Songs From The Joker Is Wild and A Hole In The Head
Capitol EAP 1-20815 Aug 1966

Golden Moments
Reprise REP 30071 Nov 1966

Strangers In The Night
Reprise REP 30077 Feb 1967

Somethin' Stupid (two tracks only)
Reprise REP 30082 Jun 1967

Yes Sir, That's Sinatra
Reprise REP 30085 Oct 1967

The World We Knew
Reprise REP 30087 Feb 1968

Christmas Mem'ries
Reprise K 14458 Nov 1978

Albums

Songs For Young Lovers
10" Capitol LC 6654 Mar 1954
Reissued on 12" ED 260074-1 (Jun 1984) and
CD 260074-2 (Feb 1988)

Sing And Dance With Frank Sinatra
10" Philips BBR 8003 Oct 1954

Swing Easy
10" Capitol LC 6689 Nov 1954
Reissued on 12" W 587 (Oct 1960) and ED 280081-1 (Jun 1984) plus CD 280081-2 also on Music For Pleasure CD CDMFP 5973 (Oct 1992)

Fabulous Frank
10" Philips BBR 8038 Feb 1955

Young At Heart (with Doris Day)
10" Philips BBR 8040 Feb 1955

In The Wee Small Hours Vol. 1
10" Capitol LC 6702 Jul 1955

In The Wee Small Hours Vol.2
10" Capitol LC 6705 Aug 1955

Songs For Swingin' Lovers
Capitol LCT 6106 Jun 1956, also on SLCT (Jul 1971)
Reissued on CD CDP 746570-2 (Mar 1987)

Conducts Tone Poems In Colour
Capitol LCT 6111 Nov 1956

High Society Soundtrack (with others)
Capitol LCT 6116 Nov 1956
Reissued on SLCT 6116 (Nov 1961)

This Is Sinatra
Capitol LCT 6123 Feb 1957
Reissued SLCT 6123 (Jul 1971) and on CD CDP 74650-2
(Mar 1988)

Close To You
Capitol LCT 6130 May 1957
Reissued on ED 2601381 (Jul 1984), World Record Club T
545 (Sep 1966), MFP 1415 (Jan 1971) and Capitol ED
2601381 (Jul 1984) plus CD CDP 746572-2 (Mar 1988)
with extra tracks

Frankie
Philips BBL 7168 Jul 1957
Reissued as Frank Sinatra on Realm RM 52062 (Sep 1965)

A Swingin' Affair
Capitol LCT 6130 Sep 1957
Reissued on CAPS 2600171 (Mar 1984) and CD CDP
794518-2 (Mar 1991) with extra track

Doris And Frank (with Doris Day)
Philips BBL 7137 Oct 1957

Christmas Dreaming
10" Philips BBR 8114 Nov 1957
Reissued as Have Yourself A Merry Little Christmas on
Hallmark HM 521 (1967) and CBS 460464-1 (Sep 1987)
plus CD 463105-2 (Nov 1989)

A Jolly Christmas From Frank Sinatra
Capitol LCT 6144 Nov 1957
Reissued as The Sinatra Christmas Album on E-ST 894
(Oct 1974), on CASPS 1809871-1 (Nov 1983) and MFP
5797 (Sep 1987) plus CD Capitol CDP 748329-2
(Nov 1987) with extra tracks, plus CD MFP CDMFP 5797
(Nov 1991)

That Old Feeling
Philips BBL 7180 Dec 1957

Pal Joey Soundtrack (with others)
Capitol LCT 6148 Jan 1958
Reissued on World Record Club ST 948 (Jan 1970) and
Vine VMP: 1005 (Oct 1975)

The Voice
Fontana TFL 5000 Jan 1958
Reissued on CBS Cameo 32520 (Oct 1984)

Where Are You?
Capitol LCT 6152 Feb 1958, also on SLCT 6152 (Jul 1959)
Reissued on CAPS 2600181 (Mar 1984) and CDP 791209-
2 (Mar 1991)

Adventures Of The Heart
Fontana TFL 5006 Mar 1958
Reissued on CBS Cameo 32319 (Aug 1983)

This Is Sinatra Vol.2
Capitol LCT 6155 May 1958
Reissued on EMS 1238 (Mar 1987) also as Frank Sinatra on
World Record Club ST 967 (May 1970)

Come Fly With Me
Capitol LCT 6154 Sep 1958, also on SLCT 6154
Reissued on ED 2600951 and CD CDP 748469-2 (Mar
1988) with extra tracks.

The Frank Sinatra Story
Fontana TFL 5030 Nov 1958

Put Your Dreams Away
Fontana TFL 5048 Mar 1959

Sings For Only The Lonely
Capitol LCT May 1959, also on SLCT 6168 (Apl 1959)
Reissued on ED 2601139 (Jul 1984) and CD CDP
7484712 (Feb 1988)

Come Dance With Me
Capitol LCT 6179 May 1959, also on SLCT 6179
(Jun 1959)
Reissued on ED 260080-1 (Sep 1984) and CD CDP
748458-2 (Mar 1984) also on CD ED260080-2 (Feb 1988)
and CD CDP 748468-2 (Nov 1992) with extra tracks

The Broadway Kick
Fontana TFL 5054 Jun 1959

Look To Your Heart
Capitol LCT 6181 Aug 1959
Reissued on ED 2601401 (Jul 1984)

No One Cares
Capitol LCT 6185 Nov 1959, also on SLCT 6185 (Jun 1960)
Reissued on World Record Club ST/T 868 (May 1969),
Capitol ED 260141-1 and CD ED 260141-2 (Jul 1984) plus
CD 794519-2 (Mar 1991) with extra tracks

Love Is A Kick
Fontana TFL 5074 Jan 1960
Reissued on Cameo 32736 (Mar 1986)

Come Back To Sorrento
Fontana TFL 5082 May 1960
Reissued as The Romantic Sinatra on Realm RM 52087
(Jan 1966)

Can Can Soundtrack (with others)
Capitol SW 1301 Jun 1960
Reissued on World Record Club T746 (Sep 1968)

Reflections
Fontana TFL 5107 Nov 1960

Nice'n'Easy
Capitol SW/W 1417 Jan 1961
Reissued on ED 2601421 (Sep 1984) and MFP 5258 (Mar
1972) plus CD 791149-2 (1988)

Sinatra Souvenir
Fontana TFL 5138 May 1961

Look Over Your Shoulder
World Record Club TP81 Jun 1961

When Your Lover Has Gone
Encore ENC 101 Aug 1961

Sinatra's Swingin' Session
Capitol SW/W 1491 Sep 1961
Reissued on ED 2602461 (Sep 1984) and CD CDP
746573-2 (Mar 1987) with extra tracks

Sinatra Swings
Reprise R1002 Oct 1961

Ring-A-Ding-Ding
Reprise R1001 Nov 1961

Sinatra Plus
Fontana SET 303 Dec 1961

Come Swing With Me
Capitol SW/W 1594 Jan 1962
Reissued on ED 2601801 (Sep 1984) also on CD CZ 391
(Mar 1991)

I Remember Tommy
Reprise R1003 Mar 1962

Sinatra And Strings
Reprise R1004 May 1962

Point Of No Return
Capitol SW/W 1676 Jul 1962
Reissued on ED 2601777-1 (Sep 1984), CD ED 2601777-2
(Feb 1988) and CD CDP 748334-2
(Nov 1992) with extra tracks.

London By Night
Capitol T 20389 Aug 1962

Sinatra Sings Great Songs From
Great Britain
Reprise R1006 Oct 1962

Sinatra And Swingin' Brass
Reprise R1005 Nov 1962
Reissued on K44192, then on Valiant VS 144

All The Way
Capitol SW/W 1538 Nov 1962
Reissued on World Record Club T570 (May 1967), Capitol
ED 260191 (Sep 1984) and CD CDP 791-150-2 (Apl 1989)

Sinatra Sings Of Love And Things
Capitol SW/W 1729 Jan 1963
Reissued on World Record Club ST/T 706 and Capitol ED
26022781 (Sep 1984)

Sinatra-Basie
Reprise R1008 Feb 1963

The Great Years 3-LP set
Capitol W1/2/3 -1762 Apl 1963
Reissued as His Greatest Years on Starline SRSSP 1/2/3
(Nov 1970)

All Alone
Reprise R1007 Jun 1963

Frank Sinatra Sings Rodgers And Hart
Capitol W 1825 Jun 1963
Reissued on Starline SRS 5083 (Nov 1971)

The Concert Sinatra
Reprise R1009 Jun 1963
Reissued on K 44001 (Jul 1971) also on CD 901009-2
(Oct 1986)

Sinatra's Sinatra
Reprise R1010 Sep 1963
Reissued on K 44002 (Jul 1971)

South Pacific (with others)
Reprise F2018 Feb 1964

My Funny Valentine
Capitol T 20577 Feb 1964

Sings Days Of Wine And Roses & Other
Academy Award Winners
Reprise R1011 May 1964
Reissued on K44003 (Jul 1971)

Finian's Rainbow (with others)
Reprise F2017 May 1964

Kiss Me Kate (with others)
Reprise F2015 May 1964

Robin And The Seven Hoods Soundtrack
(with others)
Reprise R2021 July 1964

Guys And Dolls (with others)
Reprise R2016 Sep 1964

It Might As Well Be Swing (with Count Basie)
Reprise R1012 Sep 1964
Reissued on K 44004 (Jul 1971) and CD 901012-2
(Oct 1986)

Twelve Songs Of Christmas (with Bing Crosby
and Fred Waring's Pennsylvanians)
Reprise R2022 Nov 1964
Reissued on K 34013 as White Christmas (Nov 1972)

Softly As I Leave You
Reprise R1013 Feb 1965

Singing And Swinging
Capitol W 20652 May 1965

Tell Her You Love Her
Capitol ST/T 1919 Aug 1965

September Of My Years
Reprise R1014 Sep 1965
Reissued on K 44009 (Jul 1971) and CD 901014-2
(Oct 1986)

Sinatra '65
Reprise R6167 Oct 1965

The Connoisseur's Sinatra
Capitol T 20734 Dec 1965

My Kind Of Broadway
Reprise R1015 Feb 1966

Sinatra: A Man And His Music double-LP
Reprise R 1016 Feb 1966
Reissued on K64001 (Jul 1971) and CD 901-1016-2

Sinatra For The Sophisticated
Capitol T 20757 Mar 1966

Moonlight Sinatra
Reprise R1018 May 1966

The Summit (with others)
Reprise R5031 May 1966

Strangers In The Night
Reprise R1017 July 1966
Reissued on K 44006 (Jul 1971) and CD 901017-2
(Nov 1986)

In Concert: Sinatra At The Sands
(with Count Basie)
Reprise RLP 019 Sep 1966
Reissued on K64002 (Jul 1971) and CD 901019-2
(Nov 1986)

Sinatra Sings Songs For Pleasure
MFP 1120 Nov 1966

That's Life
Reprise RLP1020 Mar 1967
Reissued on K 44007 (Jul 1971)

Francis Albert Sinatra - Antonio Carlos Jobim
Reprise RLP1021 Jun 1967
Reissued on K 44008 (Jul 1971)

Greatest Hits – The Early Years
CBS 66201 Jun 1967
Reissued on Embassy 31677 (Jun 1978)

When Your Lover Has Gone
World Record Club T611 Jul 1967

Frank Sinatra
Reprise RLP1022 Sep 1967
Reissued on K 44009 (Jul 1971)

The Movie Songs
Capitol ST/T 2700 Sep 1967

September Song
World Record Club ST/T 635 Nov 1967

The Early Years
Hallmark HM 500 Nov 1967

Have Yourself A Merry Little Christmas
Nov 1967

Francis Albert Sinatra – Edward K Ellington
Reprise RLP1024 Mar 1968
Reissued on K44010 (Jul 1971)

Frank Sinatra's Greatest Hits
Reprise RLP1025 Oct 1968
Reissued on K44011 (Jul 1971)

Someone To Watch Over Me
Hallmark SHM 592 Oct 1968

The Best Of Frank Sinatra
Capitol ST 21140 Nov 1968

The Essential Frank Sinatra Vol.1
CBS 63172 Nov 1968

The Essential Frank Sinatra Vol.2
CBS 63173 Nov 1968

The Essential Frank Sinatra Vol.3
CBS 63174 Nov 1968

Cycles
Reprise RLP1027 Feb 1969
Reissued on K44013 (Jul 1971)

My Way
Reprise RLP1029 Jun 1969
Reissued on K44015 (Jul 1971) and CD 901019-2
(Nov 1986)

Sunday And Every Day
MFP 1324 Jul 1969

A Man Alone – The Words And Music Of Rod McKuen
Reprise Sep 1969 RLP 1030
Reissued on K44016 (Jul 1971)

The Sinatra Family Wish You A Happy Christmas
Reprise RLP1026 Sep 1969

Sinatra Sings The Select Cole Porter
Starline SRS 5009 Nov 1969
Reissued on CD CDP 796611-2 (Aug 1991)

The Sinatra Touch
6-LP set World Record Club SM 137-142 Nov 1969

Watertown
Reprise RLP1031 Apl 1970
Reissued on K44017

Frank Sinatra's Greatest Hits Vol.2
Reprise RSLP1032 Nov 1970
Reissued on K44018

Sinatra And Company
Reprise RSLP1033 May 1971
Reissued on K44155 (Jul 1971)

The Sinatra Collection
Reprise R44145 Oct 1971

Sings Rodgers And Hart
Starline SRS 5083 Nov 1971

Swingin' Sinatra
2-LP Double-Up DUO 102 Oct 1972

Frank (I Remember Tommy/Sinatra And Strings)
2 LP-set Reprise K64016 Jul 1973
Reissued on K54063 (Apl 1976)

Sinatra Sings Mercer
Starline SRS 5167 Oct 1973

Ol' Blue Eyes Is Back
Reprise K44249 Nov 1973
Reissued on CD 902-115-2 (Nov 1986)

Love
MFP SPR 90039 Jul 1974

Some Nice Things I've Missed
Reprise K54020 Aug 1974

The Very Best Of Frank Sinatra
Capitol E-ST 23256 Sep 1974

The Main Event
Reprise K54031 Nov 1974

The Best Of Ol' Blue Eyes
Reprise K54042 May 1975

One For My Baby
MFP 50089 Jun 1975

The Two Originals Of Frank Sinatra (Ring-A-Ding-Ding/Sinatra Swings)
2-LP set Reprise K 84004 Aug 1976

Frank Sinatra Classics
CBS 88133 Jan 1977

The Reprise Years - 4 LP box set
Reprise K 94003 Feb 1977

Sinatra Swings
MFP 50312 Feb 1977

Portrait Of Sinatra
Double-LP Reprise K64039 Mar 1977

In The Wee Small Hours
Capitol CAPS 1008 Oct 1977
Reissued on CD CD CDP 746571-2 (Mar 1987)

Frank Sinatra's 20 Golden Greats
EMI EMTV 10 May 1978
Reissued on CD CDP 7985212 (May 1992)

The Rare Sinatra
Capitol E-ST 24311 Dec 1978
Reissued on MFP 5856 (Mar 1989)

Trilogy
3-LP set Reprise K64042 Apl 1980

In The Beginning
Double-LP CBS 22108 Sep 1980

The Screen Sinatra
Capitol CAPS 1038 Sep 1980
Reissued on MFP 5835 and CD CDMFP 5835 (Sep 1988) plus MFP CD CDMFP 6052

When Your Love Has Gone
Encore ENC 101 Aug 1981

20 Classic Tracks
MFP 50530 Nov 1981
Reissued on CD CDMFP 50530 (Mar 1992)

The Sinatra Touch
4-LP set World Record Club ALBUM 47 Nov 1981

She Shot Me Down
Reprise L54117 Jan 1982

L.A. Is My Lady
Qwest 925145-1 and CD 925145-2 Aug 1984

Songs For Young Lovers (with extra tracks)
Capitol ED 2600741 Jun 1984

Broadway Kick/Adventures Of The Heart
Double-LP CBS 22182 Jun 1985

Frank Sinatra: The Capitol Years
20 LP box set
Capitol SINATRA 20 Oct 1985

New York New York (Greatest Hits)
Warner Bros WX32 and CD 923927-2 Mar 1986

The Frank Sinatra Collection
EMI EMTV 41 Sep 1986, and CD CDP 748616-2
(Dec 1987)

The Voice 1942-1952
Double-LP CBS 450222-1 Nov 1986, and CD 450222-2
(Jun 1987)

Sinatra Swings
CBS 4600136-1 Jun 1987

Sinatra Stage
CBS 460014-1 Jun 1987

Sinatra Screen
CBS 460015-1 Jun 1987

Sinatra Love Songs
CBS 460016-1 Jun 1987

Sinatra Standards
CBS 460017-1 Jun 1987

Saloon Songs
CBS 460018-1 Jun 1987

Songs For Young Lovers/Swing Easy
CD Capitol CDP 7484702 Feb 1988

Rarities
CBS 485165-1 and CD 465165-21989 May 1989

The Great Films And Shows
Box Set Capitol FS 1 and CD CDFS 1 May 1989

The Very Best Of Frank Sinatra
Arcade CD 357 061 Aug 1989

The Capitol Collectors Series
CD Capitol CDP792160-0 Sep 1989, also on Minidisc 792160-3 (Feb 1993)

The Reprise Years
Reprise 759926501-2 and CD 759926501-2 Feb 1991

Hello Young Lovers
CD Columbia 460166-2 Aug 1991

Twenty Golden Greats
CD Capitol CDEMTV 10 May 1992

Sinatra (Soundtrack to the CBS-TV mini-series)

The Best Of The Capitol Years
Minidisc Capitol 799225-3 Feb 1993

At The Movies
CD Capitol 799374-2 Apl 1993

The Complete Columbia Recordings
12 CD Box Set Columbia CD 48673

Nov 1993 Duets
Capitol CD CDEST 2218 Dec 1993

Greatest Hits - The Early Years
CD Sony 902128-2 Jun 1994

The V-Discs - The Columbia Years
Sony Legacy 2-CD C2K 66135 Oct 1994
Contains This Sinatra, This Sinatra Vol.2 and Look To Your Heart

Duets 2
Capitol CD CDEST 2245 Nov 1994

The Sinatra Christmas Album
CD Reprise 936245743-2 Nov 1994